THE ART OF

SAUSAGE MAKING

COOKBOOK FOR BEGINNERS

FROM GROUND TO GRILL:

A BEGINNER'S COOKBOOK FOR HOMEMADE SAUSAGE CREATIONS.

Over 70 Sausage Recipes and Everything You Need to Know

About Sausage Crafting.

★★★★★

Welcome to our book on sausage making! We're grateful you've chosen to join us on this culinary journey. We value your opinion and would greatly appreciate it if you could take a moment to leave a review. Your feedback helps us improve and inspires others to embark on their own sausage-making adventures. Thank you for your support, and we hope you enjoy the book!

TABLE OF CONTENT

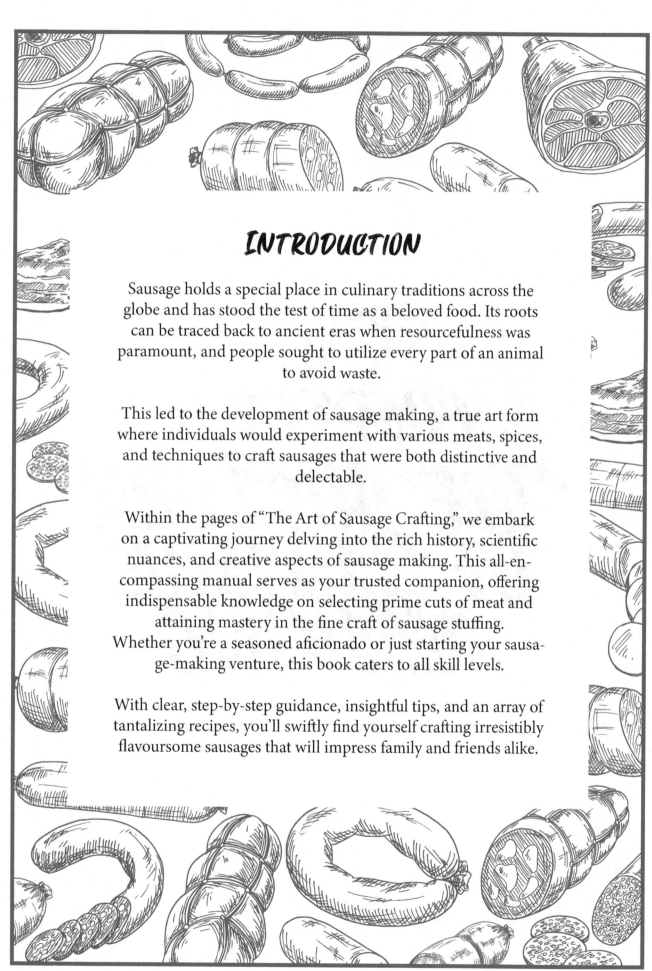

INTRODUCTION

Sausage holds a special place in culinary traditions across the globe and has stood the test of time as a beloved food. Its roots can be traced back to ancient eras when resourcefulness was paramount, and people sought to utilize every part of an animal to avoid waste.

This led to the development of sausage making, a true art form where individuals would experiment with various meats, spices, and techniques to craft sausages that were both distinctive and delectable.

Within the pages of "The Art of Sausage Crafting," we embark on a captivating journey delving into the rich history, scientific nuances, and creative aspects of sausage making. This all-encompassing manual serves as your trusted companion, offering indispensable knowledge on selecting prime cuts of meat and attaining mastery in the fine craft of sausage stuffing. Whether you're a seasoned aficionado or just starting your sausage-making venture, this book caters to all skill levels.

With clear, step-by-step guidance, insightful tips, and an array of tantalizing recipes, you'll swiftly find yourself crafting irresistibly flavoursome sausages that will impress family and friends alike.

CHAPTER 1: THE HISTORY OF SAUSAGE MAKING

Sausages have been a cherished food for centuries, with a rich history that stretches back to ancient civilizations like the Greeks, Romans, and Egyptians. In this chapter, we'll embark on an exciting journey to explore the origins and evolution of sausage making.

Origins of Sausage Making

Pinpointing the exact origins of sausage making is a challenge, as it likely developed independently in different parts of the world. However, there are fascinating theories surrounding its creation and purpose.

One theory suggests that sausages were initially crafted as a means of preserving meat. Before the advent of refrigeration, people sought ingenious ways to prevent meat from spoiling. Mixing meat with salt and other spices, then encasing it in casings for storage, proved to be an effective preservation technique.

Another theory proposes that sausages were born out of resourcefulness, a way to utilize leftover meat that might otherwise go to waste. By grinding and blending various cuts of meat, along with organs and less popular parts, people discovered a delicious and nutritious solution to repurpose these ingredients.

Ancient Sausage Making

The ancient Greeks and Romans left behind evidence of their sausage-making prowess, with references found in their literature. The Greeks delighted in "lukániko," a pork-based sausage, while the Romans enjoyed a range of varieties such as "lucanica" and "botulus."

Sausage making was also a prevalent practice in ancient Egypt. Mummified sausages unearthed from tombs dating back to approximately 3100 BC reveal the widespread consumption of sausages among both the elite and commoners.

Exploring the ancient techniques and practices of sausage making is a captivating endeavour. Ancient civilizations developed innovative methods to preserve and transform meat, allowing them to savour this delectable food even in times of scarcity.

Throughout this chapter, we'll dive into the remarkable history of sausage making, uncovering ancient traditions that shaped the craft. From the ancient civilizations of Mesopotamia and Egypt to the vibrant culinary heritage of the Roman Empire and beyond, we'll travel through time to uncover the origins of sausage making.

Ancient sausage-making techniques were driven by practicality and preservation. Salt, a highly prized commodity, played a vital role in inhibiting bacterial growth and extending the shelf life of sausages. Smoking and drying were also employed to enhance preservation and infuse unique flavours.

We'll explore the diverse range of sausages that emerged from different cultures and regions throughout history. From the bold and aromatic sausages of ancient Rome to the air-dried delicacies of Mediterranean countries, each culture contributed its distinct style and flavour to the tapestry of sausages.

Moreover, we'll examine the role of sausages in ancient culinary practices and rituals. Sausages often held symbolic significance, being offered as sacrifices to deities or enjoyed during festive occasions and communal gatherings. These traditions shed light on the cultural importance and social aspects associated with sausage making in ancient times.

This chapter will unravel ancient recipes and techniques, offering insights into the ingredients, spices, and methods employed by our ancestors to create their beloved sausages. We'll explore their innovative use of various meats, including pork, beef, poultry, and game meats, combined with an array of herbs, spices, and regional ingredients.

Understanding the roots of sausage making allows us to develop a deeper appreciation for this culinary tradition and the craftsmanship involved. It inspires us to draw inspiration from ancient techniques and flavours, enriching our own sausage-making journey with a fusion of tradition and innovation.

Join us on this captivating exploration of ancient sausage making as we unearth the secrets of the past and forge a profound connection with the timeless art of crafting sausages.

Sausage Making in the Middle Ages

During the Middle Ages, sausage making continued to thrive as an integral part of European cuisine. Different regions developed their own distinctive styles of sausages, often utilising local ingredients and spices.

Germany, in particular, saw a surge in sausage popularity during this era, and many classic German sausage varieties that are still enjoyed today originated during this time. Some notable examples include "bratwurst," "weisswurst," and "knackwurst," among others.

Industrialisation and Modern Sausage Making

The advent of industrialisation in the 19th century revolutionised sausage making, making it a more efficient and streamlined process. Cutting-edge technologies like meat grinders and sausage stuffers enabled mass production on an unprecedented scale.

Today, sausage making thrives as a vibrant industry, offering an incredible variety of sausage types and flavours worldwide. Many enthusiasts also relish the experience of crafting their own sausages at home, whether by embracing traditional methods or employing modern equipment.

From ancient times to the present day, sausage making has captivated our taste buds and enriched culinary traditions. Its enduring popularity stands as a testament to the skill, creativity, and sheer delight that go into crafting this beloved food.

CHAPTER 2: THE BASICS OF SAUSAGE MAKING

Sausage making is an enjoyable and satisfying culinary pursuit that can be embraced by individuals passionate about food. Whether you possess advanced culinary skills or are a novice in the kitchen, familiarizing yourself with the fundamentals of sausage making is a fantastic way to broaden your culinary repertoire and leave a lasting impression on your loved ones.

Within this chapter, we will comprehensively cover all the essential aspects required to embark on your sausage-making journey, encompassing necessary equipment, key ingredients, and the fundamental steps involved in crafting sausages.

Essential Equipment for Sausage Making

The specific equipment necessary for sausage making may vary depending on the approach you choose to adopt. Numerous methods exist, ranging from traditional practices employing manual tools to contemporary techniques leveraging electric machinery.

Here are some fundamental tools and equipment you will require:

Meat grinder: A pivotal component for sausage making, a meat grinder allows you to finely grind the meat to achieve the desired consistency and texture.

Sausage stuffer: This apparatus is utilized to neatly stuff the meat mixture into the casings.

Casings: Casings, which can be either natural or synthetic, are employed to encase and hold the meat mixture in place.

Kitchen scale: Precise ingredient measurement is paramount, and a kitchen scale is indispensable for this purpose.

Mixing bowls: Mixing bowls are employed to thoroughly combine the ingredients before grinding.

Knives: A quality set of knives is essential for trimming the meat and preparing the ingredients.

Thermometer: To guarantee the safety and doneness of the meat, a thermometer is crucial for monitoring the meat's temperature.

Ingredients for Sausage Making

The ingredients employed in sausage making can vary depending on the type of sausage you aim to create. However, certain foundational ingredients are commonly utilized, including:

Meat: The primary component of sausages, meat selection encompasses a wide range, such as pork, beef, chicken, or even game meats.

Fat: To achieve sausages' distinct succulent and tender texture, fat is essential. Though pork fat is often preferred, alternatives like beef fat or other types of fat can also be utilised.

Salt: Salt enhances the sausage's flavour profile while aiding in preservation.

Spices: A variety of spices and herbs are incorporated to bestow the sausages with their characteristic taste, such as paprika, garlic, fennel, and coriander.

Liquid: Some recipes may incorporate liquids like beer or wine to augment the overall flavour profile of the mixture.

Fundamental Steps in Sausage Making

The foundational steps involved in crafting sausages encompass the following:

1.Prepare the meat: Begin by trimming the meat, removing any bones or undesirable elements. Cut the meat into small pieces and chill it in the refrigerator until ready for grinding.

2.Grind the meat: Utilize a meat grinder to achieve the desired consistency during the grinding process. Maintaining a cool temperature for both the meat and the grinder is crucial to prevent fat from melting.

3.Mix the ingredients: Thoroughly combine the ground meat with the other ingredients in a mixing bowl, utilizing either your hands or a spoon.

4.Stuff the sausage: Connect the sausage stuffer to the grinder and fill the casings with the meat mixture. Tie off the casings at regular intervals to create individual sausages.

5.Cook the sausage: Sausages can be cooked utilizing various methods, such as grilling, frying, or baking. Ensure that the sausages are cooked thoroughly to guarantee they are safe for consumption.

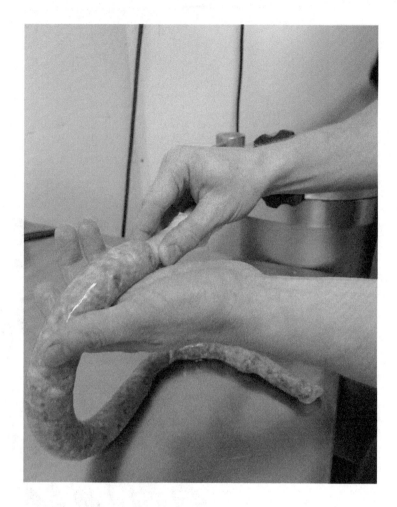

By adhering to these steps, you will be well-equipped to embark on your sausage-making endeavours, unleashing your creativity in the kitchen and relishing the joy of crafting delectable homemade sausages.

CHAPTER 3: INGREDIENTS FOR SAUSAGE MAKING

Sausage crafting is an age-old culinary tradition deeply rooted in history, transcending geographical boundaries. While the precise ingredients and techniques employed may differ across regions, the fundamental process of amalgamating ground meat, fat, seasonings, and other elements to fashion a delectable and satisfying sausage remains universally cherished.

In recent times, there has been a resurgence of interest in homemade sausages, driven by the desire to exercise control over the quality and origin of one's sustenance. Crafting sausages in the comfort of your own kitchen allows for exploration and experimentation with diverse flavour profiles, enabling the tailoring of ingredients to personal preferences. However, it is worth noting that the process of making sausages at home can be intricate and time-consuming, demanding meticulous attention to detail and the use of superior-grade ingredients.

Within this chapter, we shall delve into the core ingredients utilized in sausage making, appreciating their significance in producing sausages of exceptional quality and unparalleled taste. From the meticulous selection and preparation of meat and fat to the discerning choice of seasonings and curing agents, each ingredient assumes a pivotal role in the final outcome. Additionally, we shall explore the distinct types of casings employed in sausage making and their profound impact on both texture and flavour.

By cultivating a comprehensive understanding of the significance of each ingredient and adhering to appropriate techniques, you can fashion bespoke sausages that are as extraordinary as they are flavoursome. Now, let us embark on this tantalizing journey and explore the captivating realm of sausage making!

3.1 The Art of Selecting Meat

The selection of meat for sausage making allows for a wide spectrum of choices, wherein flavour, texture, and nutritional composition come into play. The specific meat used can vary depending on the culinary tradition and recipe under consideration. Historically, sausages were fashioned using readily available meat, often comprising leftovers or trimmings from other meat preparations. In contemporary times, premium cuts of meat, such as pork, beef, chicken, and even game meats like venison or wild boar, have become the preferred choices for most sausages.

When selecting meat for sausage making, it is imperative to opt for a cut that strikes a delicate equilibrium between fat and lean meat. The fat content is indispensable in bestowing sausages with succulence and flavour, while lean meat imparts structure and texture. Generally, the fat content should constitute approximately 30-40% of the meat's total weight.

Some popular cuts of meat employed in sausage making encompass:

Pork shoulder: Commonly referred to as pork butt, this cut is prized in sausage making owing to its elevated fat content and rich flavour.
Beef chuck: Another sought-after cut for sausage making, beef chuck strikes a balance between leanness and adequate fat, resulting in a juicy sausage.
Chicken thighs: Although less fatty compared to pork or beef, chicken thighs serve as an excellent option for those desiring a lighter sausage.
Venison: Game meats like venison offer a unique and flavourful twist when employed in sausage making.

After selecting the meat, proper preparation is paramount prior to grinding. This typically entails trimming away excess fat and connective tissue, and subsequently cutting the meat into small pieces conducive to the grinding process. Certain recipes may recommend partially freezing the meat before grinding, as this aids in maintaining optimal texture by mitigating excessive warmth.

When it comes to grinding the meat, utilizing a top-quality meat grinder specifically designed for sausage making is crucial. This ensures the meat is ground to the desired consistency while eliminating any unwanted connective tissue or gristle.

All in all, the meticulous selection and preparation of meat constitute vital steps in crafting sausages that exude exceptional quality, tantalizing flavour, and impeccable texture. By opting for cuts that strike a harmonious balance between fat and lean meat, and by meticulously preparing the meat, you can guarantee that your sausages will be juicy, flavoursome, and boast the perfect texture.

3.2 The Fat:

Let's examine the second important element in sausage making: fat.
Fat plays a vital role in sausage preparation as it contributes to moisture, flavour, and binding of ingredients. However, it is essential to use the appropriate amount and type of fat to ensure a high-quality sausage.

When selecting the fat for sausage making, it is important to choose a variety with a mild flavour and low melting point. This ensures even melting during cooking without overpowering the other ingredients. Popular options include pork fatback, beef suet, or even chicken skin.

Regarding the quantity of fat, most sausage recipes recommend a fat content of approximately 30-40% of the total meat weight. However, the exact amount depends on the recipe and personal preference. Some recipes may call for varying amounts of fat to achieve the desired texture and flavour.

Fat not only adds flavour and moisture but also aids in binding the ingredients together. It forms an emulsion when mixed with the meat and other components, ensuring cohesiveness during cooking. Insufficient fat can result in dry and crumbly sausages. However, caution should be exercised not to use excessive fat, which can lead to greasy or oily sausages. Additionally, using fat that is too warm or melting can result in a greasy or rubbery texture.

When incorporating fat into the sausage mixture, it is important to cut it into small pieces for even distribution. Some recipes may recommend grinding the fat separately before adding it to the meat mixture, while others may call for grinding the fat and meat together.

In summary, fat is a crucial ingredient in sausage making, providing moisture, flavour, and cohesion. By selecting the right type and amount of fat and ensuring proper preparation, you can create delicious sausages with the perfect texture.

3.3 The Art of Seasoning:

Seasonings are the secret behind the unique flavour and personality of sausages. They can be crafted from a diverse array of herbs, spices, and other elements, allowing you to tailor them to your specific taste preferences.

Salt, pepper, paprika, garlic, onion, and fennel are among the most widely used seasonings in sausage making. Additional options include thyme, sage, rosemary, cumin, coriander, and mustard seed.

When incorporating seasonings into your sausage mixture, it is crucial to measure them precisely and blend them thoroughly to ensure even distribution. You can grind whole spices into a fine powder using a spice grinder or mortar and pestle, or opt for pre-ground spices for convenience.

The quantity of seasonings to use depends on your personal taste and the specific recipe. It's advisable to begin with a modest amount of seasoning and adjust it gradually, tasting the mixture along the way.

When incorporating fresh herbs into your sausage mixture, make sure to finely chop them to achieve even distribution. In cases where fresh herbs aren't available, dried herbs can be used as an alternative. However, bear in mind that dried herbs have a more concentrated flavour than fresh ones, so adjust the quantity accordingly.

Apart from herbs and spices, you can introduce other ingredients to enhance the flavour of your sausages. For example, red wine or vinegar can provide a tangy note, while honey or maple syrup can add a touch of sweetness.

When selecting seasonings for your sausage, it's essential to consider the overall flavour profile you aim to achieve. For instance, if you're creating Italian sausages, a combination of fennel, garlic, and red pepper flakes can generate a bold and spicy taste.

In conclusion, seasonings play a vital role in sausage making, bestowing them with their distinct flavour and character. By skillfully choosing the right blend of herbs, spices, and additional ingredients, and adjusting the seasoning quantities to your personal preferences, you can craft sausages that are truly exceptional and delightful.

3.4 The Role of Casings:

Let's talk casings, the unsung heroes of sausage making! They play a crucial role in keeping all that filling in place and shaping those juicy sausages. In the old days, casings were all about using animal intestines, but now we have a whole range of options, both natural and synthetic.

Natural casings are crafted from the intestines of awesome animals like pigs, sheep, and cattle. They come in different sizes and shapes, depending on the kind of sausage you're whipping up. If you're after bite-sized breakfast links, hog casings are your go-to. But for those big and bold salamis, beef middles are the real stars.

Why do many sausage makers adore natural casings? Well, they give that traditional vibe and texture we all crave. Plus, they let that smoky goodness and other flavors seep right into the sausage. But hey, let's be real here—they can be a tad trickier to handle compared to synthetic casings. You gotta give 'em some extra TLC, making sure they're squeaky clean and prepped to perfection.

Synthetic casings, on the other hand, are made from fancy materials like cellulose, collagen, and plastic. They come in all sorts of sizes, shapes, and colors, and work like magic for both cooked and dry-cured sausages. Commercial sausage makers are huge fans 'cause they're consistent in size and quality, and don't need as much prep as natural casings.

Cellulose casings, made from plant-based goodies, are popular for cooked sausages like hot dogs and frankfurters. They're edible and can be easily peeled off before chowing down. Collagen casings, derived from animal connective tissues, shine in larger sausages like bologna and summer sausage. Remember, though, they're not for munching on—they need to be removed before eating. Lastly, we have plastic casings, crafted from materials like polyethylene, perfect for smoked and dry-cured sausages.

But wait, there's more! Some sausage pros even venture into alternative casings made from things like fibrous or protein films. These fancy casings come into play for larger sausages like ham and are designed to be peeled off before devouring.

In the end, choosing the right casing boils down to the sausage you're making, your personal taste buds, and what's available. Both natural and synthetic casings have their pros and cons, so pick wisely to ensure a lip-smacking, top-quality final product.

3.5 The liquid

Liquid ingredients play a pivotal role in sausage making, influencing the texture, flavour, and overall excellence of the end product. Understanding the significance of liquids empowers you to create sausages that are succulent, well-seasoned, and downright delicious. Let's embark on a journey through the realm of liquids and their importance in the art of sausage making.

Moisture Retention: Liquids like water, stocks, or broths serve as moisture retainers, ensuring sausages remain tender and juicy during cooking.
Moisture plays a key role in enhancing the succulence and juiciness of the sausages, making each bite an enjoyable experience.

Texture Enhancement: Liquids contribute to binding the ingredients together, granting sausages a cohesive texture and preventing them from crumbling.
They also lend a smoother consistency, making it easier to handle and shape the sausages with finesse.

Flavour Distribution: Liquids act as carriers, distributing seasonings, herbs, spices, and other flavourings evenly throughout the sausage mixture.
By incorporating liquids infused with aromatic ingredients, you can elevate the taste profile of your sausages to new heights.

Choosing the Right Liquids

Water: Water reigns as the most common liquid used in sausage making. It is easily accessible and provides necessary moisture without overpowering the flavour.Using cold water is essential to maintain the desired temperature during the mixing process.

Stocks and Broths: Stocks and broths, such as chicken, beef, or vegetable, add depth of flavour to sausages. They not only introduce moisture but also impart a rich savoury taste, enhancing the overall flavour profile.

Wine and Beer: Wine and beer offer the opportunity to infuse unique flavours into sausages. For instance, red wine can bring richness and complexity, while beer contributes malty or hoppy notes.When incorporating alcoholic liquids, consider their alcohol content and adjust the ratio accordingly to avoid overpowering the flavours.

Fruit Juices: Fruit juices, like apple or citrus, lend a subtle sweetness and tanginess to sausages, perfectly complementing certain flavour profiles such as pork or poultry sausages.

Tips and Considerations

Balancing Moisture Content: Striking the right balance of liquids is crucial in sausage making. Insufficient moisture can yield dry and crumbly sausages, while excessive moisture can affect the texture and binding properties.Follow recipe guidelines and adjust the liquid content as needed, taking into account factors such as fat content and meat-to-fat ratio.
Experimenting with Flavours: Embrace your creativity and experiment with various liquids to create unique

and exciting flavour combinations. Consider exploring different stocks, broths, wines, or fruit juices. Keep a record of your experiments to replicate successful results and refine your recipes.

Quality and Hygiene: Ensure the liquids used in sausage making are of high quality and safe for consumption. If utilizing homemade stocks or broths, follow proper cooking and storage practices to minimize any risks of foodborne illnesses.

3.6 Binders:

Binders play a vital role in enhancing the texture, moisture retention, and binding properties of sausages. Understanding the significance of binders empowers you to create sausages that are well-formed, succulent, and a delight to savor. So, let's delve into the realm of binders and explore their importance in the art of sausage making.

The Role of Binders in Sausage Making

Texture Enhancement: Binders, such as breadcrumbs, oats, or rice, contribute to the texture of sausages by absorbing moisture and creating a cohesive mixture.
They prevent sausages from becoming dry or crumbly, elevating the overall eating experience.
Moisture Retention: Binders assist in retaining moisture in sausages by absorbing and holding onto liquids like water or stocks. This ensures that the sausages remain juicy and succulent, even after cooking.
Binding Properties: Binders act as a binding agent, keeping the ingredients together and preventing sausages from falling apart during cooking. They improve the structural integrity of sausages, allowing them to maintain their shape and form.

Common Binders Used in Sausage Making

Breadcrumbs: Breadcrumbs are widely used as binders in sausage making.
They absorb excess moisture, provide structure to the sausage mixture, and contribute to its texture. Breadcrumbs can also lend a light, fluffy consistency.

Oats: Rolled oats or oatmeal can be employed as binders, particularly in healthier or leaner sausage variations.
Oats add a nutty flavor, enhance the texture, and improve moisture retention.

Rice: Cooked rice, whether white or brown, can serve as a binder in sausages.
Rice aids in moisture retention, contributes to a tender texture, and adds a subtle sweetness to the sausages.

Potato Starch or Flour: Potato starch or flour can be utilized as binders, especially in gluten-free recipes.
They enhance texture, moisture retention, and binding properties.

Tips and Considerations

Choosing the Right Binder: Consider the type of sausage being made, desired texture, and flavor profile. Experiment with different binders to find the one that best suits your preferences and the specific recipe.
Proper Incorporation: Ensure that the binder is evenly distributed throughout the sausage mixture. Thoroughly mix the binder with the other ingredients, using gentle but firm motions, to create a cohesive mixture.
Adjusting Binder Quantities: The required amount of binder may vary depending on the recipe, meat-to-fat ratio, and other ingredients. Begin with the recommended quantity and adjust as needed to achieve the desired texture and moisture retention.

CHAPTER 4: THE ART OF GRINDING

Grinding plays a vital role in the creation of sausages, as it transforms raw meat into the desired texture, be it fine or coarse. In this chapter, we will delve into the art of grinding, exploring the necessary equipment, techniques, and considerations that will help you achieve the perfect consistency and texture in your sausages. So, let's embark on this journey and unravel the secrets of grinding in sausage making.

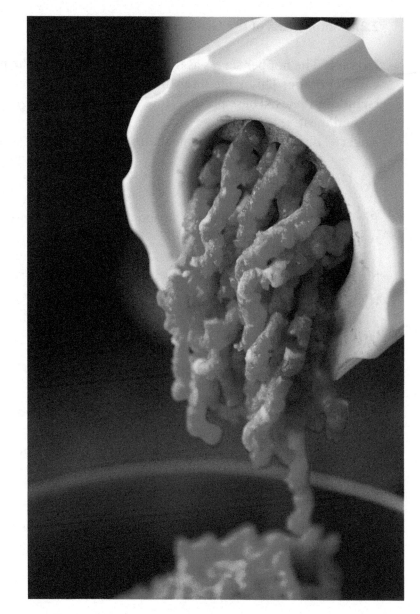

1: The Significance of Grinding

1.1. Texture Mastery: Grinding empowers you to have full control over the texture of your sausages, whether you prefer a smooth and fine texture or a rustic and coarser one.
The texture greatly influences the mouthfeel and overall eating experience of the sausage.

1.2. Ingredient Harmony: Through grinding, you ensure the even distribution of ingredients throughout the sausage mixture.
This process blends seasonings, spices, and other components uniformly, resulting in a harmonious and well-balanced flavour profile.

1.3. Fat Distribution: Proper grinding facilitates the even distribution of fat within the sausage mixture, culminating in a moist and succulent final product.
Fat distribution contributes to the juiciness and richness that defines a delightful sausage.

2: Equipment and Techniques

2.1. Grinder Varieties:

Manual Grinders: These traditional grinders require manual effort and are perfect for small-scale sausage making projects.

Electric Grinders: Powered grinders offer convenience and speed, making them suitable for larger batches or frequent usage.

2.2. Components of the Grinder:

Hopper: The hopper serves as the container that holds the meat before it enters the grinding mechanism.
Cutting Blade: This blade slices the meat into smaller pieces during the grinding process.
Grinding Plates: These plates feature holes of varying sizes, determining the fineness or coarseness of the ground meat.
Auger: The auger propels the meat through the grinding plates.

2.3. Grinding Techniques:

Pre-Chilling: By chilling the meat and grinder parts before grinding, you maintain a consistent temperature and prevent fat smearing.

Single Pass vs Multiple Passes: Depending on your desired texture, you can grind the meat once for a coarser texture or multiple times for a finer grind.

3: Tips and Considerations

3.1. Meat Selection: Select fresh and high-quality cuts of meat for grinding purposes.

Combine lean meat with fattier cuts to achieve the desired fat content in your sausages.

3.2. Temperature Control: Maintain cold temperatures for the meat and equipment throughout the grinding process. Cold temperatures help preserve the texture, prevent fat smearing, and reduce the risk of bacterial growth.

3.3. Cleaning and Maintenance: Regularly clean and maintain your grinder to ensure optimal performance and adherence to hygienic standards.

Disassemble the grinder parts, thoroughly wash them, and sanitize them before and after each use.

3.4. Embrace Experimentation: Don't hesitate to experiment with different grinding techniques and combinations of meat cuts. Adjust the size of the grinding plate and the number of passes to attain the desired texture and consistency.

Grinding stands as a pivotal step in the art of sausage making, allowing you to masterfully control the texture, achieve ingredient harmony, and ensure ideal fat distribution. By understanding the equipment, techniques, and considerations involved in grinding, you can elevate your sausage making skills to new heights.

CHAPTER 5: THE SCIENCE OF EMULSIFICATION

Section 1: Undestanding Emulsification

1.1. The Science of Emulsion:
Emulsification is the art of harmoniously blending two liquids that don't naturally mix, like fat and water, into a stable mixture. In the realm of sausage making, emulsification involves skillfully combining fat, water, and other ingredients to achieve a consistently smooth texture.

1.2. The Power of Emulsifiers:
Emulsifiers, such as proteins and phosphates, play a crucial role in creating and stabilizing the emulsion. They promote a strong bond between fat and water molecules, ensuring they stay together throughout the cooking process.

1.3. Advantages of Emulsification: Emulsification elevates the texture, moisture retention, and overall indulgence of sausages.

It guarantees a uniform distribution of fat and water, resulting in succulent and juicy sausages.

Section 2: Techniques for Perfect Emulsification

2.1. Selecting the Right Meat: Opt for meats with a higher fat content, like pork shoulder or belly, as they facilitate better emulsion formation. The fat acts as a vital lubricant, ensuring the stability of the emulsion.

2.2. Grinding and Mixing: Meticulous grinding and thorough mixing are key to achieving a homogeneous blend. Finely grind the meat to increase its surface area, promoting efficient binding of fat and water. Thoroughly mix the ingredients, ensuring their even distribution and consistent emulsification.

2.3. Temperature Control: Maintain a chilly environment by keeping the meat, fat, and equipment as cold as possible during the emulsification process. Low temperatures prevent the fat from melting and the emulsion from breaking.

2.4. Embrace High-Speed Mixing: Harness the power of high-speed mixers or food processors to create a finely blended emulsion. The rapid movement of the blades aids in breaking down fat globules, facilitating emulsion formation.

Section 3: Emulsifiers and Essential Ingredients

3.1. Harness the Power of Proteins: Proteins, such as egg whites, soy protein concentrate, or milk powder, act as natural emulsifiers in sausage making. They form a protective film around fat droplets, preventing them from coming together and stabilizing the emulsion.

3.2. The Magic of Phosphates: Phosphates, such as sodium phosphate or sodium citrate, contribute to enhanced emulsification by adjusting the pH and ionic balance.

They boost water retention capacity and improve the sausage's texture.

3.3. Unlocking Extra Potential: Non-fat dry milk, starches, and gums also contribute to emulsification, enhancing stability and texture in sausages.

Section 4: Troubleshooting Emulsion Challenges

4.1. Conquering Emulsion Breakage: Emulsion breakage can occur due to factors like improper temperature, excessive mixing, or insufficient emulsifiers.
Troubleshoot by adjusting the temperature, remixing with additional emulsifiers, or regrinding the mixture.

4.2. Preventing Fat Smearing: Fat smearing can happen when fat separates from the emulsion during grinding or mixing. To prevent smearing, maintain a cold environment, handle the meat and equipment with care, and employ proper grinding techniques.

Understanding the principles and techniques behind emulsification empowers you to craft sausages that are moist, tender, and bursting with flavor.

Embrace the science, experiment with various emulsifiers and ingredients, and refine your skills in the art of emulsification.

With practice and an adventurous spirit, you'll achieve emulsion perfection and relish in the culinary wonders you create.

CHAPTER 6:
THE ART OF STUFFING:
MASTERING THE PERFECT SAUSAGE FILLINGS

The stuffing process is where you bring your sausage mixture to life, infusing it with flavours, textures, and aromas that tantalize the taste buds. In this chapter, we will explore the artistry behind stuffing, from selecting the right casings to achieving consistent and evenly filled sausages.

Get ready to elevate your sausage making skills and delight in the joy of creating exquisite fillings. Let's begin our journey into the world of stuffing.

Section 1: Casings and Their Selection

1.1. Natural Casings: Natural casings, made from animal intestines, offer a traditional and authentic touch to sausages.

They provide a tender bite, a natural curve, and allow for proper airflow during cooking.

1.2. Synthetic Casings: Synthetic casings, such as collagen or cellulose, offer convenience and consistency. They come in various sizes and can be suitable for different sausage types.

1.3. Selecting the Right Casing: Consider the type of sausage, desired texture, cooking method, and personal preference when choosing casings.

Experiment with different casings to discover the ones that best complement your fillings.

Section 2: Techniques for Stuffing

2.1. Preparing the Casing: Soak natural casings in water to soften and remove excess salt.
Follow the manufacturer's instructions for preparing synthetic casings.

2.2. Stuffing Equipment: Sausage stuffers, both manual and electric, provide precise control and consistent filling.

Choose a stuffer that suits your needs and volume of sausage production.

2.3. Filling the Sausage: Attach the casing to the stuffer and begin feeding the sausage mixture into the stuffer's cylinder.

Maintain a steady and even pressure to ensure consistent filling and avoid air pockets.

2.4. Linking and Twisting: After filling the casing, twist it at regular intervals to create individual sausages. Practice proper linking techniques to achieve uniform-sized sausages.

Section 3: Flavourful Fillings and Techniques

3.1. Seasonings and Spices: Experiment with a variety of seasonings, herbs, and spices to create unique flavour profiles. Consider the type of sausage, regional influences, and personal preferences when selecting ingredients.

3.2. Texture Enhancers: Incorporate ingredients like breadcrumbs, rice, or cooked grains to add texture and moisture to the filling. Balance the ratios to achieve the desired consistency.

3.3. Mix-Ins and Additions: Explore the possibilities of adding diced vegetables, cheeses, nuts, or dried fruits to your fillings. These additions can provide bursts of flavour, contrasting textures, and visual appeal.

3.4. Blending and Mixing: Thoroughly combine all the ingredients to ensure even distribution of flavours and textures. Mix the filling gently to avoid overworking the meat, which can result in a dense or tough texture.

Section 4: Troubleshooting and Tips

4.1. Preventing Bursting: Avoid overstuffing the casings to prevent bursting during cooking. Leave some space for expansion and secure the ends properly.

4.2. Eliminating Air Pockets: Ensure a steady and consistent flow of the filling to reduce the chances of air pockets. Prick any visible air pockets with a needle or pin to release trapped air.

4.3. Uniform Filling Distribution: Maintain a constant pressure while filling the sausages to achieve even distribution of the mixture.

Pay attention to the thickness and consistency of the filling to ensure uniformity.

By selecting the right casings, perfecting the techniques, and exploring a myriad of flavour combinations, you can elevate your sausages to new heights.

Embrace the creative possibilities, experiment with different ingredients, and enjoy the satisfaction of crafting sausages with perfect fillings.

CHAPTER 7:
THE IMPORTANCE OF TEMPERATURE CONTROL

1: The Importance of Temperature Control

In the world of sausage making, temperature control holds the key to success. It's a vital factor that can make or break the quality of your sausages.

Properly managing temperatures throughout the sausage making process ensures food safety, optimizes texture and flavor development, and prevents undesirable outcomes.

Join us in this chapter as we explore the significance of temperature control and dive into the various stages of sausage making where temperature plays a crucial role.

Prepare to become a temperature control master as we unveil the secrets to crafting perfect sausages. Let's embark on this temperature-driven journey.

2: Temperature's Role at Each Stage

2.1. Meat Preparation: Start by ensuring the meat is chilled to the appropriate temperature before grinding.
Keeping it cold minimizes the risk of bacterial growth and helps maintain the integrity of the fat.

2.2. Grinding and Mixing: Maintain a chilly environment during grinding and mixing to prevent fat smearing and emulsion breakdown.
Keep your equipment and ingredients chilled to preserve texture and prevent fat from melting.

2.3. Stuffing: Cold temperatures are crucial during stuffing to prevent overstuffing and casing breakage.
Chilled meat and equipment help maintain consistency and prevent the emulsion from breaking.

2.4. Cooking and Smoking: Follow recommended cooking temperatures for proper food safety and to eliminate any pathogens.
Monitor the temperature during smoking to achieve the desired level of smoke flavor without compromising texture.

3: Tools for Temperature Control

3.1. Thermometers: Use reliable and accurate thermometers to measure the internal temperature of sausages during cooking. Instant-read or digital thermometers are invaluable tools for ensuring food safety and doneness.

3.2. Cold Storage: Make use of refrigeration or cold storage facilities to maintain ingredient freshness and sausage quality. Store ingredients and sausages at recommended temperatures to prevent spoilage.

3.3. Cooking Equipment: Invest in high-quality cooking equipment like ovens, smokers, or grills that offer precise temperature control. Regularly calibrate the equipment to ensure accurate temperature readings.

4: Tips for Effective Temperature Control

4.1. Time and Temperature Monitoring: Keep a close eye on duration and temperature at each stage of sausage making. Maintain a record of time and temperature to track progress and ensure consistency.

4.2. Pre-Chill Ingredients and Equipment: Pre-chill ingredients, tools, and equipment before starting the sausage making process. This ensures that the temperature remains within the desired range throughout.

4.3. Adjusting Temperatures: Be ready to make adjustments based on ambient temperature, sausage type, and desired outcome. Increase or decrease cooking temperature or adjust cooking time accordingly to achieve desired results.

Temperature control is a critical aspect of sausage making that impacts food safety, texture, and flavor development. By understanding its role at each stage, equipping yourself with reliable tools, and implementing effective control techniques, you can elevate your sausage making skills to new heights.

Embrace the importance of temperature control as a key ingredient in creating sausages that are safe, succulent, and bursting with flavor. With diligence and precision, you'll achieve mastery over temperature, and your sausages will consistently impress and satisfy.

CHAPTER 8: SMOKING AND CURING TECHNIQUES

1: The Craft of Smoking

1.1. Smoking Techniques:

Smoking is a time-honored method that infuses sausages with distinct flavors. Two primary methods are commonly used:

Cold Smoking: This technique involves smoking sausages at temperatures below 30°C (86°F) for an extended period. It imparts a delicate smoky flavor without fully cooking the sausages.

Hot Smoking: In hot smoking, sausages are exposed to both smoke and heat simultaneously. This method cooks the sausages while infusing them with rich, smoky flavors.

1.2. Smoke Sources:

The choice of smoke sources greatly influences the final flavor profile of sausages. Consider the following options:

Wood Chips: Different types of wood chips, like hickory, apple, or cherry, provide unique smoke flavors. For example, hickory imparts a robust and bacon-like smokiness, while applewood offers a mild and fruity aroma.

Wood Pellets: Pellet smokers have gained popularity for their convenience and ability to provide consistent smoke. Pellets made from various woods allow precise control over the intensity and duration of smoke.

1.3. Temperature and Time:

Maintaining the perfect smoking temperature is crucial for successful sausage making. Consider the following:

Maintain the ideal smoking temperature, typically between 70°C and 90°C (158°F and 194°F), depending on the specific type of sausage.

Smoking time varies based on factors such as sausage size, thickness, desired smokiness, and personal preference.

2: The Art of Curing

2.1. Dry Curing:

Dry curing involves applying a mixture of salt, sugar, and spices to draw out moisture and create a preserved, flavorful product. Here are key points to consider:
Evenly coat the sausages with the curing mixture to ensure consistent flavor throughout.
Place the cured sausages in a controlled environment, like a refrigerator, and periodically turn them to facilitate the even distribution of flavors.

2.2. Wet Curing:

Wet curing, also known as brining, involves immersing the sausages in a solution of water, salt, sugar, and spices. Consider the following:
Fully submerge the sausages in the brine to allow the flavors to penetrate the meat.
Store the sausages in a refrigerator during the curing process to develop flavors and allow the meat to absorb the brine.

2.3. Considerations:
Pay attention to the following considerations when curing sausages:
Use high-quality salts, such as kosher or sea salt, without additives or anti-caking agents, for a clean and natural curing process.
Precisely measure curing ingredients to maintain the desired balance of flavors in the sausages.

Section 3: Key Factors to Consider

3.1. Smoke Intensity: Controlling the intensity of smoke is crucial for achieving desired flavors in smoked sausages. Consider the following factors:

Smoke Density: Adjust the amount of smoke generated during the smoking process to avoid overpowering or subtle flavors.
Smoke Duration: Determine the optimal smoking duration based on sausage size, thickness, desired smokiness, and personal preference.

3.2. Temperature Control: Maintaining precise temperature control is vital during smoking and curing. Consider the following:

Smoking Temperature: Monitor and maintain the ideal smoking temperature range, typically between 70°C and 90°C (158°F and 194°F), for proper cooking and smoke absorption.
Curing Temperature: Maintain a consistent temperature during the curing process, following specific guidelines for the chosen method.

3.3. Resting Period: Allow sausages to rest after smoking or curing before consumption. This resting period enhances flavors and redistributes moisture for improved taste and texture.

Smoking and curing techniques are ancient arts that have stood the test of time in sausage making. By understanding these techniques, you can elevate your sausages to new levels of flavor and preservation. Embrace the aromas and tastes that smoking and curing bring, and experiment with different methods, wood types, and spices to create your signature sausages.

With practice and a passion for the craft, you'll master the art of smoking and curing, transforming ordinary sausages into culinary masterpieces. Enjoy the satisfaction of creating delicious, smoky sausages that will tantalize the taste buds and impress your friends and family.

CHAPTER 9: TYPE OF SAUSAGES

From traditional favourites to regional specialties, sausages offer a wide range of flavours, textures, and cooking methods. Whether you're a meat lover, a fan of international cuisine, or simply curious about expanding your culinary horizons, this chapter will be your guide to understanding and appreciating the diverse world of sausages.

Section 1: Fresh Sausages

Breakfast Sausages:

- **Description:** Breakfast sausages are small, typically pork-based sausages seasoned with a delightful blend of herbs and spices. They are commonly enjoyed alongside breakfast staples like eggs, bacon, and toast.
- **Flavor Profile:** Mild, savory, with a hint of sweetness and subtle spices.
- **Cooking Method:** Breakfast sausages are usually pan-fried, grilled, or baked until they reach an internal temperature of 165°F (74°C).

Italian Sausage:

- **Description:** Italian sausages are coarse-ground pork sausages seasoned with a delightful mix of herbs and spices, such as fennel, garlic, and paprika. They come in both sweet (mild) and hot varieties.
- **Flavor Profile:** Bold, aromatic, with a prominent fennel and garlic taste.
- **Cooking Method:** Italian sausages can be grilled, pan-fried, or used as an ingredient in pasta dishes, pizzas, and sandwiches.

Bratwurst:

- **Description:** Bratwurst is a German sausage made with a combination of pork and veal, or sometimes just pork. It is seasoned with a blend of spices, such as marjoram, nutmeg, and white pepper.
- **Flavor Profile:** Juicy, mildly seasoned, with a touch of sweetness and nuttiness.
- **Cooking Method:** Bratwursts are often grilled, pan-fried, or simmered in beer before being served in a bun with sauerkraut or mustard.

Section 2: Cooked and Smoked Sausages

2.1. Frankfurter:

- **Description:** Frankfurters, commonly known as hot dogs, are made from finely ground beef or pork, mixed with spices, and encased in a natural or synthetic casing.
- **Flavor Profile:** Mild, salty, smoky, with a hint of garlic and spices.
- **Cooking Method:** Frankfurters are usually boiled, grilled, or pan-fried and served in a bun with various toppings.

2.2. Polish Kielbasa:

- **Description:** Polish Kielbasa is a popular smoked sausage made from coarsely ground pork, seasoned with garlic, marjoram, and other spices.
- **Flavor Profile:** Rich, smoky, garlicky, with a well-rounded blend of spices.
- **Cooking Method:** Polish Kielbasa is traditionally smoked and can be enjoyed grilled, pan-fried, or simmered in soups and stews.

2.3. Chorizo:

- **Description:** Chorizo is a highly seasoned sausage originating from Spain, made from coarsely ground pork and seasoned with paprika, garlic, and various spices.
- **Flavor Profile:** Spicy, smoky, tangy, with a distinct paprika and garlic taste.
- **Cooking Method:** Chorizo can be grilled, pan-fried, or used as an ingredient in various dishes, such as paella, tapas, or Mexican cuisine.

Section 3: Dry-Cured Sausages

3.1. Salami:

- **Description:** Salami is a type of dry-cured sausage that originated in Italy. It is made from finely ground pork, seasoned with a blend of spices, and fermented and air-dried for weeks or months.
- **Flavor Profile:** Rich, savory, tangy, with a complex blend of spices and a distinctive fermented taste.
- **Serving Method:** Salami is typically enjoyed thinly sliced as part of charcuterie boards, sandwiches, or antipasto platters.

3.2. Pepperoni:

- **Description:** Pepperoni is a popular dry-cured sausage commonly used as a pizza topping. It is made from finely ground pork and beef, seasoned with spices, such as paprika, garlic, and cayenne pepper.
- **Flavor Profile:** Spicy, tangy, smoky, with a pronounced paprika and garlic flavor.
- **Serving Method:** Pepperoni is commonly sliced and used as a pizza topping but can also be enjoyed in sandwiches or as a snack.

From traditional breakfast sausages to delectable dry-cured varieties, sausages offer a world of culinary delights waiting to be explored. By understanding the unique characteristics and cooking methods of different sausages, you can unlock a world of flavors and create memorable dining experiences.

CHAPTER 10: TROUBLESHOOTING AND TIPS

In this chapter, we'll address common challenges that can arise during the sausage making process and provide valuable tips to overcome them. From texture issues to flavor inconsistencies, we'll delve into the art of problem-solving to ensure your sausage-making journey is smooth and successful. Let's explore the world of troubleshooting and useful tips, so you can create perfect sausages every time.

Texture Issues

1.1. Dry or Crumbly Texture:

Possible Causes:

Insufficient fat content in the meat mixture.
Overmixing or excessive grinding, resulting in a loss of fat emulsion.
Inadequate binding agents or moisture retention.

Troubleshooting Tips:

Ensure the correct fat-to-lean meat ratio, typically around 30% fat to 70% lean meat, to achieve the desired texture.

Avoid excessive grinding or overmixing the meat, as it can break down the fat and result in a drier texture. Incorporate binders or moisture-retaining ingredients, such as breadcrumbs or powdered milk, to enhance moisture retention.

1.2. Tough or Rubber-like Texture:

Possible Causes:

Overmixing or excessive grinding, resulting in overworked proteins.
Insufficient fat content or poor fat distribution.
Improper cooking or smoking techniques.

Troubleshooting Tips:

Avoid excessive mixing or grinding, as it can lead to protein extraction and result in a tough texture.
Ensure an adequate fat content and proper distribution throughout the meat mixture.
Follow appropriate cooking or smoking techniques, including maintaining the correct temperature and cooking duration.

Flavor Issues

2.1. Lack of Seasoning:

Possible Causes:

Underseasoning during the mixing stage.
Insufficient marinating or resting time.

Troubleshooting Tips:

Ensure proper seasoning during the mixing stage, using precise measurements and adjusting to personal taste preferences.

Allow adequate marinating or resting time to allow the flavors to develop and permeate the meat.

2.2. Off or Bitter Flavor:

Possible Causes:

Over-smoking or excessive smoke exposure.
Poor quality or spoiled ingredients.
Inadequate temperature control during cooking or smoking.

Troubleshooting Tips:

Monitor the intensity of smoke during the smoking process to prevent the sausages from becoming overly smoky or bitter.
Use fresh and high-quality ingredients to avoid off flavors.
Ensure proper temperature control during cooking or smoking to avoid unpleasant flavors.

General Tips

3.1. Equipment and Ingredient Preparation:

Ensure all equipment and utensils used in sausage making are clean and properly maintained.
Prepare ingredients in advance, including proper meat chilling, spice measurement, and ingredient organization.

3.2. Recipe Testing and Adjustment:

Conduct small-scale recipe testing before scaling up to larger batches.
Keep detailed records of ingredients, measurements, and procedures for future reference and adjustments.

3.3. Temperature Control and Food Safety:

Maintain proper temperature control throughout the sausage making process, from meat storage to cooking and smoking.

Follow food safety guidelines to prevent contamination and ensure safe consumption.

Troubleshooting and incorporating useful tips are essential elements of successful sausage making. By understanding common texture and flavor issues and implementing the appropriate troubleshooting techniques, you can overcome challenges and create sausages that have perfect texture, flavor, and quality.

Remember to pay attention to ingredient preparation, seasoning, temperature control, and equipment maintenance to ensure consistent results.

CHAPTER 12: SAUSAGE STORAGE AND PRESERVATION

Properly storing your homemade sausages is essential for maintaining their quality, safety, and freshness. Whether you plan to enjoy them right away or save them for later, understanding the principles of sausage storage is crucial. Let's explore some best practices to ensure your sausages stay delicious.

1. Refrigeration

1.1. Temperature and Humidity: Keep sausages in the refrigerator between 0°C and 4°C (32°F to 40°F) to prevent bacterial growth.

Maintain a humidity level of approximately 85% in the refrigerator to prevent drying out.

1.2. Packaging: Individually wrap sausages in plastic wrap or use airtight containers to protect them from air and odours.

Label each package with the sausage type and preparation date for easy identification.

1.3. Shelf Life: For optimal quality, consume fresh sausages within 2 to 3 days of preparation. Cooked sausages can be refrigerated for up to 4 to 5 days, but it's best to enjoy them sooner.

2. Freezing

2.1. Freezer Temperature: Set your freezer temperature to -18°C (0°F) or below to maintain the quality and safety of frozen sausages.

Use a freezer thermometer to ensure proper temperature control.

2.2. Freezing Packaging: Wrap sausages tightly in freezer-grade plastic wrap, removing air to prevent freezer burn.

Place wrapped sausages in freezer bags or airtight containers for additional protection.

2.3. Freezer Shelf Life: Raw sausages can be frozen for 2 to 3 months without significant loss of quality. Cooked sausages can be frozen for 2 to 3 months, but it's best to consume them within 1 to 2 months.

3. Sausage Preservation Techniques

3.1. Drying and Curing: EDry-cured sausages like salami or pepperoni require specific curing methods involving salt, seasonings, and controlled humidity.

Follow established recipes and guidelines for safe and successful dry curing.

3.2. Smoking: Smoking is a popular preservation method that adds flavour and extends the shelf life of sausages. Smoke sausages at low temperatures using wood chips or pellets for a smoky aroma and enhanced preservation.

3.3. Vacuum Sealing: Vacuum sealing is an effective technique for extending the shelf life of sausages by removing air and preventing oxidation.
Use a vacuum sealer and appropriate bags for optimal preservation.

CHAPTER 13: SAUSAGE MAKING EQUIPMENT

In our exploration of sausage making equipment, we will discuss a variety of options, their functions, and how to select the most suitable ones for your needs. Let's delve into the world of sausage-making tools!

1. Grinding Equipment

1.1. Types of Grinders:
Electric Meat Grinder: These powerful machines are perfect for large-scale sausage making, offering different grinding speeds and cutting plate sizes.
Manual Meat Grinder: Ideal for smaller batches and occasional use, these affordable hand-cranked grinders are easy to operate.

1.2. Grinder Components and Functions:
Hopper: The container where you place the meat for grinding.
Auger: Transfers the meat from the hopper to the grinding plates.
Grinding Plates: Come in various sizes to determine the coarseness of the ground meat.
Cutting Blades: Responsible for mincing and cutting the meat during the grinding process.
Motor (Electric Grinder): Powers the grinding process for effortless operation.
Crank Handle (Manual Grinder): Rotates the auger to manually grind the meat.

1.3. Grinding Tips:
Cut the meat into small cubes before grinding for consistent and easier results.
Keep the meat and grinder components cold to prevent the meat from warming up.
Use different grinding plate sizes to achieve the desired texture of your sausages.

2. Stuffing Equipment

2.1. Sausage Stuffers:
Vertical Stuffer: These standalone units come in various capacities and feature a vertical design for controlled and smooth sausage stuffing.

Horizontal Stuffer: Suitable for commercial settings, these powerful machines offer high-capacity stuffing capabilities.

2.2. Stuffer Components and Functions:
Cylinder: Holds the sausage mixture to be stuffed.
Piston: Pushes the sausage mixture through the stuffing tube into the casings.
Stuffing Tubes: Attach to the stuffer and determine the diameter of the sausages.

2.3. Stuffing Tips:
Keep the sausage mixture cold to prevent stickiness and facilitate handling.
Apply vegetable oil to the stuffing tubes for effortless stuffing.
Avoid overstuffing the casings to prevent bursting during cooking.

3. Casings and Accessories

3.1. Natural Casings:
Hog Casings: Excellent for traditional sausages like bratwurst and Italian sausages, providing a natural casing with great flavor and texture.
Sheep Casings: Smaller casings commonly used for breakfast sausages and cocktail-sized sausages.

Beef Casings: Sturdy casings suitable for larger sausages like bologna or salami that require longer cooking times.

3.2. Synthetic Casings:
Collagen Casings: Made from edible collagen, these casings offer a consistent diameter and work well for smoked and cooked sausages.
Cellulose Casings: Non-edible casings suitable for making larger sausages or hot dog-style sausages.

3.3. Accessories:
Sausage Prickers: Used to remove air bubbles from stuffed sausages before cooking.
Butcher Twine: Essential for tying off casings or securing stuffed sausages.

Investing in quality sausage making equipment is vital for achieving consistent, efficient, and enjoyable results. Whether it's a reliable grinder for efficient meat grinding, a versatile sausage stuffer for smooth stuffing, or high-quality casings and accessories, having the right tools at your disposal makes the sausage-making process more manageable and rewarding.

Consider your specific needs, budget, and desired sausage types when choosing your equipment, and enjoy the journey of creating delicious sausages with the help of these essential tools.

CHAPTER 11: SAUSAGE RECIPES

FRESH SAUSAGES

CLASSIC PORK SAUSAGES

Ingredients:

5 m Natural Sausage Casings
750 g Pork Blade
750 g Pork Shoulder
400 g Pork Belly Fat
125 g Bread Crumbs
3 Tbsp Dried Sage
1 Tbsp Salt
1.5 Tbsp Ground Mace
1 Tsp Sweet Paprika
1.5 Tbsp Powdered Mustard
1 Tbsp Black Pepper

Instructions:

1. Soak your sausage skins as per the instructions and rinse off any salt.

2. Chop the meat and fat into large pieces and pass through a medium plate on your meat grinder.

3. Make sure that you alternate between fat and meat to begin the mixing process.

4. Mix the herbs spices and bread crumbs into the minced meat.

5. Fry off a small pattie of sausage meat to test the seasoning and increase if you wish.

6. Feed the sausage casings onto the sausage filling attachment on to your mixer. It is ok to make childish jokes at this point!

7. Set up the meat grinder into the sausage making configuration.

8. Begin to fill the sausage skins and as soon as you can see the pork mixture beginning to show through into the skin then turn off the grinder.

9. Tie a knot into the end of the skin leaving about 5cm of the casing empty on the side of the casing with no filling

10. Then proceed with filling the sausage skins.

11. To divide the long sausage into individual portions pinch the sausage and twist.

12. When moving to the next sausage pinch again but be sure to twist in the opposite direction repeating always in the opposite direction to the previous sausage.

13. Enjoy the delicious taste of homemade Classic Pork Sausages with this simple and satisfying recipe!

CUMBERLAND SAUSAGES

Ingredients:

- 4 lbs pork shoulder
- 1 lb pork belly
- 8 oz rusk/breadcrumbs
- 16 oz water
- 5 Tbsp Kosher or sea salt
- 1 ½ Tbsp freshly ground black pepper
- 2 tsp ground nutmeg
- 2 tsp ground coriander
- 2 tsp ground mace

Instructions:

1. Grind the Meat: Cut the pork meat into chunks (size should be according to your meat grinder instructions). Once it is all cut, place into the grinder with a medium to coarse grind plate (about 5mm).

2. Season the Meat: Put half of the ground pork in a large bowl and add the salt, but be sure to use Kosher or sea salt (do not use table salt or it will be too salty). Next, add the spices.
Mix well and run through the meat grinder a second time.
Add the rest of the ground pork, and the rusk/breadcrumbs. Now add the water.
Mix well, preferably with your hands, as it is easier to incorporate everything evenly. At this point, you can fry a little of the sausage to taste it. Adjust the seasonings if necessary.
Grind once more (optional, however, we did).

3. Stuff the Sausage Meat into the Casings: Tie the end of a sausage casing. Using the sausage stuffing attachment, hold the casing over the end and start filling it with the machine.
Hold the casing on so it doesn't slide off, and gently hold the sausage as it's made so that it has a bit of a guide.
With a sharp, small skewer or toothpick, prick holes into the sausages. This is a pricking tool that my Nonno Scipione made in Italy many years ago.
Now you are ready to do one of two things: cook the sausages or freeze them. Given the large amount of sausages this recipe makes, you'll probably do what we did--a little of both.

Note: cayenne pepper can be added optionally according to personal preference.

LINCOLNSHIRE SAUSAGES

Ingredients:

- 1.7kg pork (mixture of shoulder & belly)
- 360g breadcrumbs (use fresh soft bread)
- 3tsp fine sea salt
- 1.5tsp freshly-ground black pepper
- 1tsp ground coriander
- 16 large fresh sage leaves
- 2tsp freshly-grated nutmeg
- 2tsp cornflour
- 400ml cold water
- Natural Hog Casings (casings for thick sausages)

Instructions:

1. Add the salt, pepper, coriander, sage leaves and nutmeg to the meat and mix together (you can leave to marinate/infuse for a couple of hours if you like).

2. Put through a meat grinder/mincer on a wide/chunky setting.

3. Make the breadcrumbs in a food processor, then add to the meat, herb & seasoning mixture and add the water and cornflour. Mix well by hand to ensure the flavours and all ingredients are evenly spread. The breadcrumbs and meat will absorb the water and you'll end up with a pasty/sticky mixture.

4. Thread the natural casings over your sausage maker nozzle and feed the mixture through. Do this slowly and let the sausages get as thick as you'd like them to. Work on a long continuous length for each 10-12 sausages, twisting to separate each time you've reached the desired length for one sausage.

5. You can then either refrigerate/freeze them linked as they are, or separate by cutting through at the twisting points with scissors and freezing them individually.

6. These Lincolnshire sausages are very cost-effective (ours worked out at about £0.50 per sausage to make) and you know exactly what's in them! Food doesn't get much better

LORNE SAUSAGES (SQUARE SAUSAGES)

Ingredients:

- 450g (1lb) minced beef
- 450g (1lb) minced pork
- 250g (1.5 cups) breadcrumbs (not fresh)
- 1 tsp ground black pepper
- 1 tsp salt (add to taste)
- 1.5 tsp coriander
- 0.5 tsp nutmeg
- 0.5 tsp mace
- 120ml (0.5 cups) cold water

Instructions:

1. Press the sausage meat firmly into the loaf tin, ensuring it is packed tightly. Any remaining sausage meat can be set aside to make meat patties.

2. Cover the top of the tin with clingfilm, making sure it is fully wrapped. Place the tin in the freezer for approximately 2 hours, or until the sausage meat is firm enough to slice. Alternatively, you can refrigerate it for 24 hours until it reaches the desired firmness. Note: Avoid using pre-frozen meat for this recipe, as it should only be frozen and thawed once.

3. Using the clingfilm, lift the sausage out of the tin and cut it into slices approximately 1cm thick.

4. The sliced sausage can be used immediately, refrigerated for up to 2 days, or frozen for future use. To freeze, place baking paper between the slices and store them in a container.

5. When ready to cook, heat a frying pan and cook the sausage slices for a few minutes on each side, or grill them according to your preference. Serve the cooked sausages in a morning roll with your choice of sauce, as part of a full Scottish breakfast, or even in your Stovies!

GLAMORGAN SAUSAGES

Ingredients:

- 200g Caerphilly cheese, grated
- 150g fresh breadcrumbs
- 1 medium onion, finely chopped
- 2 cloves of garlic, minced
- 2 tablespoons fresh parsley, finely chopped
- 1 teaspoon dried thyme
- 1/2 teaspoon ground nutmeg
- 2 large eggs
- 4 tablespoons milk
- Salt and pepper to taste
- Vegetable oil for frying

Instructions:

1. Melt butter in a large skillet over medium high heat. Add leek and thyme leaves and cook, stirring, until onions are soft and just beginning to brown, about 5 minutes. Remove from heat and set aside.

2. In a large bowl combine cheese, 1 cup breadcrumbs, 1 egg, milk, mustard, and reserved leek mixture. Season with salt and pepper. Mix with hands until all the ingredients are moist and you can easily form a sausage shape with the mixture. Divide mixture into 8 pieces and form each piece into the shape of a sausage.

3. Place remaining breadcrumbs, flour, and remaining beaten egg in separate plates. Bread each sausage by coating it in flour, then egg, then breadcrumbs.

4. In a high sided skillet or saucepan, heat 1-inch of oil over medium-high heat until shimmering. Cook sausages until browned on all sides, about 3 minutes total. Transfer to a paper towel-lined place and season with salt. Serve immediately.

APPLE AND SAGE BREAKFAST SAUSAGES

Ingredients:

- 1 large apple
- 1 large egg, lightly beaten
- 1/2 cup chopped fresh parsley
- 1-1/4 pounds lean ground turkey
- 6 teaspoons olive oil, divided
- 1-1/4 teaspoons salt
- 1/2 teaspoon pepper
- 1/2 teaspoon crushed red pepper flakes
- 3 to 4 tablespoons minced fresh sage
- 2 garlic cloves, minced

Instructions:

1. Start by peeling an apple and shredding it coarsely. Place the shredded apple in a colander set over a plate. Allow it to stand for 15 minutes. Then, gently squeeze and blot the shredded apple dry using paper towels.

2. In a large bowl, combine an egg, parsley, sage, garlic, seasonings, and the prepared apple. Mix these ingredients together well. Add ground turkey to the bowl and gently but thoroughly mix everything together. Shape the mixture into sixteen 2-inch patties and place them on baking sheets lined with waxed paper. Cover the patties and refrigerate them for 8 hours or overnight.

3. When you're ready to cook the patties, heat 2 teaspoons of oil in a large nonstick skillet over medium heat. Cook the patties in batches, allowing 3-4 minutes on each side or until they turn golden brown and reach an internal temperature of 165°F (74°C) according to a thermometer. Add more oil to the skillet as needed.

CHICKEN AND SPINACH SAUSAGES

Ingredients:

- 4 1/2 lbs chicken thighs (2 kg)
- 7 -10 ounces fresh spinach (1 bag)
- 5 teaspoons salt
- 2 teaspoons ground black pepper
- 2 teaspoons dried sage
- 1 teaspoon dried thyme
- 4 garlic cloves

   Notes: you can also add feta cheese for an add
   on cheesier take.

Instructions:

1. Begin by removing the bones from the chicken thighs, ensuring to leave the fat intact.

2. Slice the chicken thighs into 1-inch cubes and place them in a bowl.

3. Mince the garlic and add it to the bowl of chicken.

4. Add the remaining spices to the bowl.

5. Combine all the ingredients in the bowl thoroughly, then refrigerate the mixture for at least an hour.

6. Mince the spinach and add it to the other ingredients in the bowl.

7. Use a blender or food processor to grind all the ingredients together.

8. Using your hands, combine and mix the sausage mixture for a couple of minutes.

9. Now, you can begin stuffing the mixture into pork casings. You may use a funnel and a stick to push it down into the casings. Tie the casings and hang them in the air to dry for 1 hour.

10. The sausage can be fried or cooked and used in various pasta dishes. Enjoy!

Beef and Guinness Sausages

Ingredients:

- 500g (1.1 lbs) of beef mince (ground beef), preferably with a good fat content
- 1 small onion, finely chopped
- 2 cloves of garlic, minced
- 1/4 cup of fresh parsley, finely chopped
- 1/4 cup of fresh thyme leaves, finely chopped
- 1/4 cup of fresh rosemary leaves, finely chopped
- 1/4 cup of fresh chives, finely chopped
- 1/4 cup of Guinness beer
- 2 teaspoons of salt
- 1 teaspoon of ground black pepper
- Natural hog casings, soaked in water according to package instructions (optional)

Instructions:

1. In a large bowl, combine the ground beef and Guinness beer. Mix well until the beer is evenly distributed throughout the meat.

2. Add the salt, black pepper, garlic powder, onion powder, dried thyme, dried rosemary, dried parsley, and paprika to the bowl. Mix thoroughly to ensure that all the seasonings are well incorporated into the meat.

3. If using pork casings, rinse them under cold water and soak them in water for about 30 minutes to soften. Rinse again before using.

4. If using casings, attach them to a sausage stuffer or a funnel attached to the end of a sausage-making tube. Stuff the beef mixture into the casings, twisting the sausages into desired lengths.

5. If not using casings, shape the beef mixture into sausage patties or links with your hands.

6. Preheat a grill or heat a skillet over medium heat. Cook the sausages for about 4-5 minutes per side, or until they are fully cooked and reach an internal temperature of 160°F (71°C).

7. Once cooked, remove the sausages from the grill or skillet and let them rest for a few minutes.

8. Serve the Beef and Guinness sausages hot and enjoy them as a standalone dish or use them in your favorite recipes such as sandwiches, pasta dishes, or as part of a hearty breakfast.

LAMB MERGUEZ SAUSAGES

Ingredients:

- 2 teaspoons (6g) whole cumin seed
- 2 teaspoons (6g) whole coriander seed
- 2 teaspoons (6g) whole fennel seed
- 2 tablespoons (14g) paprika
- 2 tablespoons (18g) Diamond Crystal kosher salt, plus more to taste; for table salt use half as much by volume or the same weight
- 1 teaspoon (3g) cayenne pepper
- 3 pounds (1.4kg) lamb shoulder, cut into 3/4-inch cubes and gristle removed
- 1 pound (455g) lamb, beef, or pork fat, cut into 3/4-inch cubes
- 2 tablespoons freshly minced garlic (about 6 medium cloves; 25g)
- 1/3 cup (75g) harissa
- 1/3 cup (80ml) ice water
- Lamb casings, soaked in warm water for 30 minutes prior to use
  Notes: you can also add feta cheese for an add on cheesier take.

Instructions:

1. Toast cumin, coriander, and fennel seeds in a skillet until fragrant. Grind them into a powder and mix with paprika, salt, and cayenne.

2. Stuff the spice mixture into pork casings using a funnel and tie the casings securely. Hang them to dry for 1 hour.

3. In a bowl, combine lamb, fat, spice mixture, garlic, and harissa. Chill for 20 minutes.

4. Grind the mixture through a meat grinder and mix in a stand mixer with water until sticky and uniform.

5. Cook a small patty, adjust seasonings if needed, then stuff the mixture into lamb casings and twist into 6-inch links. Refrigerate until ready to cook.

6. Grill the sausages over medium-high direct heat until they reach an internal temperature of 155°F (68°C) when tested with an instant-read thermometer in the middle of the link. This usually takes about a few minutes per side.

7. Rest for 5 minutes before serving.

MAPLE AND BACON SAUSAGES

Ingredients:

- 500g pork mince
- 150g bacon, finely chopped
- 2 tablespoons maple syrup
- 1 teaspoon dried sage
- 1/2 teaspoon dried thyme
- 1/2 teaspoon salt
- 1/4 teaspoon black pepper
- Pork casings (optional)
- Cooking oil (for frying)

Instructions:

1. In a large bowl, combine the pork mince, chopped bacon, maple syrup, dried sage, dried thyme, salt, and black pepper. Mix well until all the ingredients are evenly incorporated.

2. If using pork casings, rinse them thoroughly and soak them in water according to the package instructions.

3. Take a small amount of the sausage mixture and shape it into a patty. Cook the patty in a frying pan over medium heat until cooked through. Taste and adjust the seasonings if needed.

4. If using casings, slide one end of the casing onto a sausage stuffer or a piping bag fitted with a large round nozzle. Fill the casing with the sausage mixture, leaving some space at the ends to tie them off.

5. Twist the filled casing at regular intervals to create individual sausages. Alternatively, if not using casings, shape the sausage mixture into patties or rolls.

6. Heat some cooking oil in a frying pan over medium heat. Add the sausages and cook until golden brown and cooked through, turning them occasionally to ensure even cooking.

7. Once cooked, remove the sausages from the pan and place them on a plate lined with kitchen paper to absorb any excess oil.

8. Serve the maple and bacon sausages hot with your preferred accompaniments, such as eggs, toast, or in a breakfast roll.

SUN-DRIED TOMATO AND BASIL SAUSAGES

Ingredients:

- 500g (1.1 lbs) of ground pork
- 1/2 cup of sun-dried tomatoes, finely chopped
- 1/4 cup of fresh basil leaves, finely chopped
- 1 small onion, finely chopped
- 2 garlic cloves, minced
- 1 teaspoon of salt
- 1/2 teaspoon of black pepper
- 1/2 teaspoon of dried oregano
- 1/2 teaspoon of dried thyme
- Natural hog casings, soaked in water according to package instructions (optional)

Instructions:

1. In a large mixing bowl, combine ground pork, finely chopped sun-dried tomatoes, fresh basil, onion, garlic, salt, black pepper, dried oregano, and dried thyme. Mix everything together to create a delicious Mediterranean flavour.

2. Ensure all the ingredients are thoroughly mixed, evenly distributing the sun-dried tomatoes and basil for a consistent taste.

3. For a smoother texture, pass the mixture through a meat grinder or food processor.

4. Shape the mixture into patties or stuff it into casings if desired. If using casings, prepare your sausage stuffer or attach the sausage stuffing attachment to your meat grinder.

5. For casings, gently fill them with the mixture, creating smooth and consistent sausages. Twist the sausages into 10-12cm (4-5 inch) links, allowing room for twisting and linking.

6. For patties, divide the mixture into equal portions and shape them into 1 cm (1/2 inch) thick discs.

7. Cook the Sun-Dried Tomato and Basil Sausages by grilling, pan-frying, or baking them in the oven. Ensure they reach an internal temperature of 70°C (160°F) for thorough cooking.

8. As the sausages cook, the aroma of sun-dried tomatoes and fragrant basil will fill your kitchen, evoking the Mediterranean atmosphere.

9. Once cooked to perfection, serve the sausages with your preferred accompaniments. They go well with fresh salads, crusty bread, and a drizzle of extra virgin olive oil. Enjoy the burst of vibrant flavours in each bite.

GARLIC AND HERB SAUSAGES

Ingredients:

- 500g (1.1 lbs) of ground pork
- 3 garlic cloves, minced
- 2 tablespoons of fresh herbs (such as parsley, thyme, and rosemary), finely chopped
- 1 teaspoon of salt
- 1/2 teaspoon of ground black pepper
- 1/2 teaspoon of paprika
- 1/4 teaspoon of dried oregano
- 1/4 teaspoon of dried basil
- Natural hog casings, soaked in water according to package instructions (optional)

Instructions:

1. In a large mixing bowl, combine ground pork, minced garlic, fresh herbs, salt, black pepper, paprika, dried oregano, and dried basil. Mix everything together for a delightful blend of garlic and herb flavours.

2. Thoroughly mix the ingredients, ensuring even distribution of the garlic and herbs throughout the pork mixture. This step is important for a well-balanced taste.

3. For a smoother texture, pass the mixture through a meat grinder or food processor to achieve a uniform consistency.

4. Once combined, shape the sausages. If using casings, prepare your sausage stuffer or attach the sausage stuffing attachment to your meat grinder.

5. Gently fill the casings with the mixture, aiming for a consistent and smooth filling. Twist the sausages into individual links, around 10-12cm (4-5 inches) long, leaving space for twisting and linking.

6. If not using casings, shape the mixture into traditional sausage shapes or form patties.

7. Now, it's time to cook these delicious Garlic and Herb Sausages. Grill, pan-fry, or bake them in the oven until they turn a beautiful golden brown. Make sure they reach an internal temperature of 70°C (160°F) for thorough cooking.

8. As the sausages cook, your kitchen will be filled with the irresistible aroma of garlic and herbs, tantalizing your taste buds.

9. Once cooked to perfection, let the sausages rest for a few minutes to allow the flavours to settle and the juices to redistribute within them.

10. Serve your Garlic and Herb Sausages with your favourite accompaniments. They go wonderfully with creamy mashed potatoes, steamed vegetables, and a refreshing green salad. Enjoy the bold flavours and savour the deliciousness of these homemade sausages.

MEDITERRANEAN LAMB SAUSAGES

Ingredients:

- 500g ground lamb
- 100g lamb fat
- 1 tsp cumin seeds
- 1 tsp coriander seeds
- 1 tsp fennel seeds
- 2 cloves of garlic, minced
- Handful of fresh mint leaves, finely chopped
- Handful of fresh parsley leaves, finely chopped
- 1 tsp salt
- Natural sausage casings

Instructions:

1. Toast cumin, coriander, and fennel seeds in a dry pan until fragrant. Let them cool, then grind into a powder.

2. Mix ground lamb and lamb fat in a bowl.

3. Add minced garlic, chopped mint leaves, chopped parsley leaves, ground toasted seeds, and salt to the lamb mixture. Mix well.

4. Stuff the mixture into natural sausage casings using a sausage stuffer or meat grinder attachment.

5. Twist the sausages into 10-12cm (4-5 inch) links. Refrigerate for a few hours if desired.

6. Grill, pan-fry, or bake the sausages until fully cooked (internal temperature of 70°C/160°F).

7. Let the sausages rest for a few minutes before serving.

8. Enjoy the Mediterranean Lamb Sausages with your favourite accompaniments.

THAI LEMONGRASS AND GINGER SAUSAGES

Ingredients:

- 500g ground pork
- 2 stalks of lemongrass, finely chopped
- 1 thumb-sized piece of ginger, grated
- 3 cloves of garlic, minced
- 2 red chillies, finely chopped
- Handful of fresh coriander leaves, finely chopped
- 1 tsp fish sauce
- 1 tsp soy sauce
- 1 tsp brown sugar
- 1/2 tsp salt
- Natural sausage casings

Instructions:

1. In a large mixing bowl, combine the ground pork, lemongrass, ginger, garlic, chillies, coriander leaves, fish sauce, soy sauce, brown sugar, and salt. Mix well to ensure all the ingredients are evenly distributed.

2. If using natural sausage casings, soak them in water according to the package instructions to soften them.

3. Attach a sausage stuffer or a sausage stuffing attachment to your meat grinder.

4. Stuff the pork mixture into the sausage casings, making sure to pack it tightly. Twist the sausages into links of your desired length, leaving some room for twisting and linking.

5. Once all the sausages are formed, refrigerate them for at least an hour to allow the flavors to meld.

6. Preheat your grill or a frying pan over medium heat. Cook the sausages for about 10-12 minutes, turning occasionally, until they are browned and cooked through.

7. Remove the sausages from the heat and let them rest for a few minutes.

8. Serve the Thai Lemongrass and Ginger Sausages with a side of steamed jasmine rice, a squeeze of lime juice, and some sweet chili sauce.

MAPLE AND SAGE BREAKFAST SAUSAGES

Ingredients:

- 500g ground pork
- 1 tablespoon maple syrup
- 1 teaspoon dried sage
- 1/2 teaspoon salt
- 1/4 teaspoon black pepper
- 1/4 teaspoon dried thyme
- 1/4 teaspoon garlic powder
- 1/4 teaspoon onion powder

Instructions:

1. In a large mixing bowl, combine the ground pork, maple syrup, dried sage, salt, black pepper, dried thyme, garlic powder, and onion powder. Mix well using your hands or a spoon until all the ingredients are evenly incorporated.

2. Take a small amount of the mixture and shape it into a small patty. Cook the patty in a frying pan over medium heat until fully cooked. Taste and adjust the seasonings in the mixture if needed.

3. Once you're satisfied with the taste, divide the mixture into equal portions and shape them into small sausage patties.

4. Heat a non-stick frying pan or skillet over medium heat. Place the sausage patties in the pan, leaving some space between them. Cook for about 4-5 minutes on each side, or until they are nicely browned and cooked through.

5. Once cooked, remove the sausages from the pan and place them on a plate lined with kitchen paper to absorb any excess oil.

6. Serve the Maple and Sage Breakfast Sausages hot alongside your favourite breakfast dishes, such as scrambled eggs, toast, or pancakes. They also go well with a side of fresh fruit or a cup of coffee.

HONEY MUSTARD SAUSAGES

Ingredients:

- 500g ground pork
- 2 tablespoons honey
- 2 tablespoons Dijon mustard
- 1 teaspoon salt
- 1/2 teaspoon ground black pepper
- 1/2 teaspoon garlic powder
- 1/4 teaspoon dried thyme
- 1/4 teaspoon paprika (optional)

Instructions:

1. In a large mixing bowl, combine the ground pork, honey, Dijon mustard, salt, black pepper, garlic powder, dried thyme, and paprika (if using). Mix well using your hands or a spoon until all the ingredients are evenly incorporated.

2. Take a small amount of the mixture and shape it into a small patty. Cook the patty in a frying pan over medium heat until fully cooked. Taste and adjust the seasonings in the mixture if needed.

3. Once you're satisfied with the taste, divide the mixture into equal portions and shape them into sausage patties.

4. Heat a non-stick frying pan or skillet over medium heat. Place the sausage patties in the pan, leaving some space between them. Cook for about 4-5 minutes on each side, or until they are nicely browned and cooked through.

5. Once cooked, remove the sausages from the pan and let them rest for a few minutes.

6. Serve the Honey Mustard Sausages hot alongside your favourite sides, such as mashed potatoes, steamed vegetables, or a fresh salad. They also go well in a bun as a tasty sausage sandwich.

JALAPENO AND CHEDDAR PATTY SAUSAGES

Ingredients:

- 500g ground pork
- 100g cheddar cheese, grated
- 2 jalapeno peppers, finely chopped (seeds removed for milder heat)
- 1 teaspoon salt
- 1/2 teaspoon ground black pepper
- 1/2 teaspoon garlic powder
- 1/4 teaspoon dried oregano
- 1/4 teaspoon smoked paprika (optional)

Instructions:

1. In a large mixing bowl, combine the ground pork, grated cheddar cheese, finely chopped jalapeno peppers, salt, black pepper, garlic powder, dried oregano, and smoked paprika (if using). Mix well using your hands or a spoon until all the ingredients are evenly incorporated.

2. Take a small amount of the mixture and shape it into a small patty. Cook the patty in a frying pan over medium heat until fully cooked. Taste and adjust the seasonings in the mixture if needed.

3. Once you're satisfied with the taste, divide the mixture into equal portions and shape them into sausage patties.

4. Heat a non-stick frying pan or skillet over medium heat. Place the sausage patties in the pan, leaving some space between them. Cook for about 4-5 minutes on each side, or until they are nicely browned and cooked through.

5. Once cooked, remove the sausages from the pan and let them rest for a few minutes.

6. Serve the Jalapeno and Cheddar Sausages hot alongside your favourite sides, such as mashed potatoes, grilled vegetables, or in a soft bun as a delicious sausage sandwich.

MUSHROOM AND SWISS BRATWURST

Ingredients:

- 1 package of No. 284 Mushroom Bratwurst Seasoning or No. 275 Blue Ribbon Bratwurst Seasoning
- 15-16 lbs. cubed pork butt
- 2 cans of mushroom pieces with stems (1 can drained, 1 can with reserved liquid)
- 5 lbs. high-temp Swiss cheese
- 10-12 cups crushed ice
- 1 package of 32-25 mm hog casings

Instructions:

1. In a large mixing bowl, combine the cubed pork butt, bratwurst seasoning, and crushed ice. Mix well before grinding the mixture.
2. Pass the mixture through a 3/16" plate using a meat grinder.
3. Add the drained mushrooms and Swiss cheese to the ground mixture. Mix thoroughly but quickly to prevent the ice from melting.

Note: It's important to work efficiently and keep the meat mixture cold throughout the process. Return the mixture to the fridge or freezer whenever possible. Similarly, refrigerate the sausage links as they are made. Cold temperatures help maintain a bright pink color and ensure the desired texture. The stuffer hopper should have condensation forming on it, indicating that the meat mix is sufficiently cold.

This recipe should yield approximately 100-110 links measuring 7 inches each when using the 32-35 mm hog casings.

TOULOUSE SAUSAGES

Ingredients:

- 2 pounds (900g) pork shoulder, cubed
- 1/2 pound (225g) pork fatback, cubed
- 2 cloves garlic, minced
- 2 teaspoons salt
- 1 teaspoon ground black pepper
- 1 teaspoon ground white pepper
- 1 teaspoon dried thyme
- 1 teaspoon dried oregano
- 1/2 teaspoon ground nutmeg
- 1/4 cup red wine

Instructions:

1. In a large bowl, combine the pork shoulder, pork fatback, minced garlic, salt, black pepper, white pepper, dried thyme, dried oregano, and ground nutmeg.

2. Mix the ingredients well using your hands or a spoon until they are evenly distributed.

3. If using a meat grinder, pass the mixture through the grinder using a medium-sized plate.

4. Alternatively, you can use a food processor to blend the mixture until it reaches a coarse texture.

5. Once the mixture is ground, add the red wine and mix it in thoroughly.

6. Prepare your sausage stuffer with natural hog casings and load the sausage mixture into the stuffer.

7. Stuff the mixture into the casings, twisting them at regular intervals to form individual sausages.

8. If you prefer not to use casings, you can shape the mixture into patties.

9. Refrigerate the sausages for at least 2 hours to allow the flavors to meld together.

10. When ready to cook, you can grill, pan-fry, or bake the sausages until they are cooked through and golden brown.

11. Serve the Toulouse Sausages with your favorite accompaniments, such as mashed potatoes, sautéed vegetables, or crusty bread.

ITALIAN SWEET SAUSAGES

Ingredients:

- 2 pounds (900g) pork shoulder, cubed
- 1/2 pound (225g) pork fatback, cubed
- 2 cloves garlic, minced
- 2 teaspoons salt
- 1 teaspoon ground black pepper
- 1 teaspoon fennel seeds
- 1 teaspoon paprika
- 1/2 teaspoon dried oregano
- 1/4 teaspoon red pepper flakes (optional)
- 1/4 cup red wine

Instructions:

1. In a large bowl, combine the pork shoulder, pork fatback, minced garlic, salt, black pepper, fennel seeds, paprika, dried oregano, and red pepper flakes (if using).

2. Mix the ingredients well using your hands or a spoon until they are evenly distributed.

3. If using a meat grinder, pass the mixture through the grinder using a medium-sized plate.

4. Alternatively, you can use a food processor to blend the mixture until it reaches a coarse texture.

5. Once the mixture is ground, add the red wine and mix it in thoroughly.

6. Prepare your sausage stuffer with natural hog casings and load the sausage mixture into the stuffer.

7. Stuff the mixture into the casings, twisting them at regular intervals to form individual sausages.

8. If you prefer not to use casings, you can shape the mixture into patties.

9. Refrigerate the sausages for at least 2 hours to allow the flavors to meld together.

10. When ready to cook, you can grill, pan-fry, or bake the sausages until they are cooked through and golden brown.

11. Serve the Italian Sweet Sausages with your favorite accompaniments, such as pasta, roasted vegetables, or a crusty Italian bread.

Note: Maintain a cold environment while working with the sausage mixture. Keep the meat and equipment chilled to ensure a proper texture and prevent the fat from melting. You can even place the mixture in the freezer for 30 minutes before grinding or stuffing.

Experiment with the seasoning quantities to suit your taste preferences.

SPICY FRESH SAUSAGE

Ingredients:

- Ingredients:
-
- 500g lean pork shoulder
- 250g pork back fat
- 15g kosher salt
- 5g paprika
- 3g crushed red pepper flakes
- 3g dried oregano
- 2g garlic powder
- 2g onion powder
- 1g ground black pepper
- 100ml ice water
- Hog casings, soaked and rinsed

Instructions:

1. Cut lean pork shoulder and pork back fat into small pieces suitable for grinding.

2. Combine kosher salt, paprika, crushed red pepper flakes, dried oregano, garlic powder, onion powder, and ground black pepper in a mixing bowl to create a spice blend.

3. Grind the pork shoulder and back fat using a medium-sized plate on a meat grinder.

4. Transfer the ground meat to a large mixing bowl and add the spice blend. Mix thoroughly.

5. Add ice water to the mixture and continue mixing until the meat becomes sticky and binds together.

6. Soak hog casings in water to make them pliable.

7. Stuff the sausage mixture into the hog casings, forming links as desired.

8. Prick the sausages with a sausage pricker to release air pockets.

9. Cook the sausages by grilling, pan-frying, or baking until fully cooked and reaching an internal temperature of 160°F (71°C).

10. Allow the sausages to rest for a few minutes before serving.

11. Enjoy your homemade spicy fresh sausages in various dishes or as a flavourful addition to your favourite recipes.

Smoky Chipotle Sausages

Ingredients:

- 800g pork shoulder, diced
- 200g pork fat, diced
- 2 chipotle peppers in adobo sauce, minced
- 3 garlic cloves, minced
- 1 tablespoon smoked paprika
- 2 teaspoons salt
- 1 teaspoon ground black pepper
- 1 teaspoon dried oregano
- 1/2 teaspoon ground cumin
- 2.5 meters of natural hog casings

Instructions:

1. In a large bowl, combine the diced pork shoulder, pork fat, minced chipotle peppers, minced garlic, smoked paprika, salt, black pepper, dried oregano, and ground cumin. Mix well to ensure the seasonings are evenly distributed.

2. Grind the mixture using a meat grinder, using a medium-sized plate.

3. Attach the sausage stuffer attachment to your meat grinder or use a sausage stuffer machine.

4. Soak the hog casings in water for about 30 minutes to soften them.

5. Slide the soaked casings onto the sausage stuffer nozzle.

6. Start filling the casings with the sausage mixture, using the sausage stuffer. Be careful not to overstuff, leaving enough space for twisting and linking.

7. Once the sausages are stuffed, twist and link them at desired intervals to form individual sausages.

8. Prick any air bubbles in the sausages with a sterilized needle to release the trapped air.

9. Heat a grill or skillet over medium heat. Cook the sausages for about 15-20 minutes, turning occasionally, until they are browned and cooked through.

10. Remove the sausages from the heat and let them rest for a few minutes before serving.

11. Serve the Smoky Chipotle Sausages hot with your favorite accompaniments, such as bread rolls, sautéed onions, or mustard.

HERB-INFUSED PORK SAUSAGES

Ingredients:

- 500g pork shoulder, trimmed and diced
- 200g back fat, diced
- 2 garlic cloves, minced
- 1 tablespoon fresh thyme leaves, finely chopped
- 1 tablespoon fresh rosemary leaves, finely chopped
- 1 tablespoon fennel seeds
- 2 teaspoons paprika
- 1 teaspoon salt
- 1/2 teaspoon ground black pepper
- Sausage casings

Instructions:

1. In a large bowl, combine the diced pork shoulder, back fat, minced garlic, thyme leaves, rosemary leaves, fennel seeds, paprika, salt, and black pepper. Mix well until all the ingredients are evenly distributed.

2. Pass the mixture through a meat grinder fitted with a medium grinding plate. This will help blend the flavors and ensure a consistent texture.

3. Soak the sausage casings in water according to the package instructions to soften them.

4. Attach a sausage stuffer or a sausage stuffing attachment to your meat grinder.

5. Stuff the pork mixture into the sausage casings, ensuring they are tightly packed. Twist the sausages into links of your desired length, leaving some room for twisting and linking.

6. Once all the sausages are formed, refrigerate them for at least an hour to allow the flavors to develop.

7. Preheat a grill or a frying pan over medium heat. Cook the sausages for about 12-15 minutes, turning occasionally, until they are golden brown and cooked through.

8. Remove the sausages from the heat and let them rest for a few minutes.

9. Serve the homemade sausages with your favorite accompaniments, such as crusty bread, mustard, or a side salad.

MOROCCAN SPICED SAUSAGES

Ingredients:

- 800g minced lamb or beef
- 200g lamb or beef fat, finely chopped
- 2 garlic cloves, minced
- 1 teaspoon ground cumin
- 1 teaspoon ground coriander
- 1 teaspoon ground cinnamon
- 1/2 teaspoon ground ginger
- 1/2 teaspoon ground paprika
- 1/2 teaspoon ground turmeric
- 1/2 teaspoon ground black pepper
- 1/2 teaspoon salt
- 2 tablespoons chopped fresh parsley
- 2 tablespoons chopped fresh coriander (cilantro)
- 2.5 meters of natural lamb or hog casings

Instructions:

1. In a large bowl, combine the minced lamb or beef, chopped lamb or beef fat, minced garlic, ground cumin, ground coriander, ground cinnamon, ground ginger, ground paprika, ground turmeric, ground black pepper, salt, chopped parsley, and chopped coriander. Mix well to evenly distribute the spices and herbs.

2. Attach the sausage stuffer attachment to your meat grinder or use a sausage stuffer machine.

3. Soak the lamb or hog casings in water for about 30 minutes to soften them.

4. Slide the soaked casings onto the sausage stuffer nozzle.

5. Start filling the casings with the sausage mixture, using the sausage stuffer. Be careful not to overstuff, leaving enough space for twisting and linking.

6. Once the sausages are stuffed, twist and link them at desired intervals to form individual sausages.

7. Prick any air bubbles in the sausages with a sterilized needle to release the trapped air.

8. Heat a grill or skillet over medium heat. Cook the sausages for about 15-20 minutes, turning occasionally, until they are browned and cooked through.

9. Remove the sausages from the heat and let them rest for a few minutes before serving.

10. Serve the Moroccan Spiced Sausages hot with couscous, salad, or pita bread.

HERBED TURKEY SAUSAGES

Ingredients:

- 800g ground turkey
- 200g turkey fat, finely chopped
- 2 cloves of garlic, minced
- 1 tablespoon chopped fresh sage
- 1 tablespoon chopped fresh thyme
- 1 tablespoon chopped fresh rosemary
- 1 teaspoon salt
- 1/2 teaspoon ground black pepper
- 1/2 teaspoon dried oregano
- 1/2 teaspoon dried basil
- 2.5 meters of natural hog or collagen casings

Instructions:

1. In a large bowl, combine the ground turkey, chopped turkey fat, minced garlic, chopped sage, chopped thyme, chopped rosemary, salt, black pepper, dried oregano, and dried basil. Mix well to evenly distribute the herbs and seasonings.

2. Attach the sausage stuffer attachment to your meat grinder or use a sausage stuffer machine.

3. Soak the hog or collagen casings in water for about 30 minutes to soften them.

4. Slide the soaked casings onto the sausage stuffer nozzle.

5. Start filling the casings with the sausage mixture, using the sausage stuffer. Be careful not to overstuff, leaving enough space for twisting and linking.

6. Once the sausages are stuffed, twist and link them at desired intervals to form individual sausages.

7. Prick any air bubbles in the sausages with a sterilized needle to release the trapped air.

8. Heat a grill or skillet over medium heat. Cook the sausages for about 12-15 minutes, turning occasionally, until they are cooked through and reach an internal temperature of 75°C (165°F).

9. Remove the sausages from the heat and let them rest for a few minutes before serving.

10. Serve the Herbed Turkey Sausages hot with your choice of sides, such as roasted vegetables, mashed potatoes, or a fresh salad.

FETA AND SPINACH SAUSAGES

Ingredients:

- 800g ground pork
- 200g pork fat, finely chopped
- 150g feta cheese, crumbled
- 100g fresh spinach, chopped
- 2 cloves of garlic, minced
- 1 teaspoon dried oregano
- 1 teaspoon dried basil
- 1/2 teaspoon salt
- 1/2 teaspoon ground black pepper
- 2.5 meters of natural hog or collagen casings

Instructions:

1. In a large bowl, combine the ground pork, chopped pork fat, crumbled feta cheese, chopped spinach, minced garlic, dried oregano, dried basil, salt, and black pepper. Mix well to evenly distribute the ingredients.

2. Attach the sausage stuffer attachment to your meat grinder or use a sausage stuffer machine.

3. Soak the hog or collagen casings in water for about 30 minutes to soften them.

4. Slide the soaked casings onto the sausage stuffer nozzle.

5. Start filling the casings with the sausage mixture, using the sausage stuffer. Be careful not to overstuff, leaving enough space for twisting and linking.

6. Once the sausages are stuffed, twist and link them at desired intervals to form individual sausages.

7. Prick any air bubbles in the sausages with a sterilized needle to release the trapped air.

8. Heat a grill or skillet over medium heat. Cook the sausages for about 12-15 minutes, turning occasionally, until they are cooked through and reach an internal temperature of 75°C (165°F).

9. Remove the sausages from the heat and let them rest for a few minutes before serving.

10. Serve the Feta and Spinach Sausages hot with your choice of sides, such as roasted vegetables, couscous, or a fresh salad.

SMOKED SANSAGES

HAWAIIAN PINEAPPLE TERIYAKI SAUSAGES

Ingredients:

- 800g ground pork
- 200g pork fat (e.g., fatback, skin removed)
- 1 cup fresh pineapple, finely chopped
- 4 tablespoons teriyaki sauce
- 2 tablespoons soy sauce
- 1 tablespoon brown sugar
- 1 teaspoon garlic powder
- 1 teaspoon onion powder
- 1/2 teaspoon ground ginger
- 1/2 teaspoon black pepper
- 2.5m sausage casings

Instructions:

1. In a large mixing bowl, combine the ground pork, pork fat, chopped pineapple, teriyaki sauce, soy sauce, brown sugar, garlic powder, onion powder, ground ginger, and black pepper. Mix well to ensure all ingredients are evenly distributed.

2. Cover the bowl with plastic wrap and refrigerate for at least 1 hour to allow the flavors to meld together.

3. Prepare the sausage casings by rinsing them thoroughly in cold water and soaking them according to the package instructions.

4. Attach a sausage stuffer nozzle to a sausage stuffer or a meat grinder with a sausage stuffing attachment.

5. Slide the soaked casing onto the nozzle, leaving a small overhang.

6. Stuff the sausage mixture into the casing, ensuring it fills evenly without any air pockets. Slowly and steadily push the mixture through, guiding the casing off the nozzle as you go.

7. Twist the sausage into individual links, about 10-12cm long, and tie off the ends.

8. Repeat the stuffing and twisting process until all the sausage mixture is used.

9. If desired, you can refrigerate the sausages overnight to further enhance the flavors.

10. Preheat your smoker to a temperature of around 110-120°C (225-250°F) using fruitwood chips for smoking.

11. Place the sausages on the smoker grates and smoke them for approximately 2-3 hours until they reach an internal temperature of 70°C (160°F).

12. Remove the sausages from the smoker and let them rest for a few minutes before serving.

13. Enjoy your homemade Hawaiian Pineapple Teriyaki Sausages as a tasty and tropical treat!

Note: If you don't have a smoker, you can also cook the sausages on a grill or in an oven using indirect heat. Just make sure to monitor the internal temperature to ensure they are fully cooked.

PORTUGUESE CHOURIÇO

Ingredients:

- Pork shoulder – 2.25 kilograms (5 pounds)
- Garlic – 5 cloves (halved)
- Kosher Salt - 25 grams
- Dry red wine – 500 ml
- Paprika - 30 grams
- Black pepper – 5 grams
- Bay leaves – 4
- Sausage casings – 5 meters (36mm – 40 mm)

Instructions:

1. Cut the pork into 10mm cubes.

2. Mix with all the other ingredients.

3. Cover with cling film and place in the refrigerator.

4. Remove every 12 hours and mix the meat with the marinade for two to three days.

5. In the 24 hours before stuffing place the casings in clean water and allow to soak in the fridge

6. Once ready to perform stuffing remove the garlic and bay leaves.

7. Rinse the casings and place in lukewarm water for 30 minutes.

8. Stuff the mixture into the casings. Tie off at regular intervals.

9. Prick the casings with a needle to remove any air pockets

10. Place into a smoker and cold smoke for 24 hours

11. Once smoked, hang the sausages to dry in a cold, dry space inside. (A spare refrigerator with hanging space works well.

12. Once dry. The sausages can be served, but still need to be cooked

SMOKED ANDOUILLE SAUSAGE

Ingredients:

- 1.5 kg pork shoulder, cut into small pieces
- 500g pork fatback, cut into small pieces
- 30g kosher salt
- 2 teaspoons paprika
- 2 teaspoons garlic powder
- 2 teaspoons onion powder
- 1 teaspoon ground black pepper
- 1 teaspoon dried thyme
- 1 teaspoon dried oregano
- 1 teaspoon cayenne pepper
- 1/2 teaspoon ground allspice
- 1/2 teaspoon ground cloves
- 2.5m hog casings

Instructions:

1. In a large bowl, mix together the pork shoulder, pork fatback, salt, paprika, garlic powder, onion powder, black pepper, thyme, oregano, cayenne pepper, allspice, and cloves until well combined.

2. Cover the bowl with plastic wrap and refrigerate for 1 hour to allow the flavours to blend.

3. Rinse the hog casings in cold water and soak them according to the package instructions.

4. Attach a sausage stuffer nozzle to a sausage stuffer or meat grinder with a sausage stuffing attachment.

5. Slide the soaked casing onto the nozzle, leaving a small overhang.

6. Stuff the sausage mixture into the casing, ensuring it fills evenly without air pockets. Guide the casing off the nozzle as you go.

7. Twist the sausage into links, about 10-12cm long, and tie off the ends.

8. Preheat your smoker to 110-120°C (225-250°F) using your preferred smoking wood chips or chunks.

9. Place the sausages on the smoker grates and smoke for 2-3 hours until they reach an internal temperature of 70°C (160°F).

10. Remove the sausages from the smoker and let them rest for a few minutes before serving.

11. Enjoy your homemade Smoked Andouille Sausage in dishes like jambalaya, gumbo, or as a flavourful addition to your favourite recipes!

SMOKED KIELBASA SAUSAGE

Ingredients:

- 1.5 kg pork shoulder, cut into small pieces
- 500g pork fatback, cut into small pieces
- 30g kosher salt
- 2 tsp ground black pepper
- 2 tsp garlic powder
- 2 tsp mustard seeds
- 2 tsp marjoram
- 1 tsp ground allspice
- 1 tsp ground coriander
- 1/2 tsp curing salt (optional)
- 2.5m hog casings

Instructions:

1. In a large bowl, combine the pork shoulder, pork fatback, salt, black pepper, garlic powder, mustard seeds, marjoram, allspice, coriander, and curing salt (if using). Mix well to evenly distribute the seasonings.

2. Cover the bowl with plastic wrap and refrigerate for 1-2 hours to allow the flavours to meld.

3. Rinse the hog casings under cold water and soak them according to the package instructions.

4. Attach a sausage stuffer nozzle to a sausage stuffer or a meat grinder with a sausage stuffing attachment.

5. Slide the soaked casing onto the nozzle, leaving a small overhang.

6. Stuff the sausage mixture into the casing, making sure to fill it evenly without air pockets. Guide the casing off the nozzle as you go.

7. Twist the sausage into links, about 10-12cm long, and tie off the ends.

8. Preheat your smoker to 110-120°C (225-250°F) using your preferred smoking wood chips or chunks.

9. Place the sausages on the smoker grates and smoke for 2-3 hours until they reach an internal temperature of 70°C (160°F).

10. Remove the sausages from the smoker and let them rest for a few minutes before serving.

11. Enjoy your homemade Smoked Kielbasa Sausage! It can be served on its own, grilled, or used in various dishes like stews, sandwiches, or with sauerkraut.

SMOKED BRATWURST SAUSAGE

Ingredients:

- 1.5 kg pork shoulder, cut into small pieces
- 500g pork fatback, cut into small pieces
- 30g kosher salt
- 2 tsp ground white pepper
- 2 tsp ground nutmeg
- 2 tsp ground ginger
- 2 tsp dried parsley
- 2 tsp powdered onion
- 2 tsp powdered garlic
- 2.5m hog casings

Instructions:

1. In a large bowl, combine the pork shoulder, pork fatback, salt, white pepper, nutmeg, ginger, dried parsley, powdered onion, and powdered garlic. Mix well to evenly distribute the seasonings.

2. Cover the bowl with plastic wrap and refrigerate for 1-2 hours to allow the flavours to meld.

3. Rinse the hog casings under cold water and soak them according to the package instructions.

4. Attach a sausage stuffer nozzle to a sausage stuffer or a meat grinder with a sausage stuffing attachment.

5. Slide the soaked casing onto the nozzle, leaving a small overhang.

6. Stuff the sausage mixture into the casing, making sure to fill it evenly without air pockets. Guide the casing off the nozzle as you go.

7. Twist the sausage into links, about 10-12cm long, and tie off the ends.

8. Preheat your smoker to 110-120°C (225-250°F) using your preferred smoking wood chips or chunks.

9. Place the sausages on the smoker grates and smoke for 2-3 hours until they reach an internal temperature of 70°C (160°F).

10. Remove the sausages from the smoker and let them rest for a few minutes before serving.

11. Enjoy your homemade Smoked Bratwurst Sausage! Serve it on a bun with mustard and sauerkraut or use it in traditional German recipes like Bratwurst with Sauerkraut and Potatoes.

SMOKED CHORIZO SAUSAGE

Ingredients:

- 800g pork shoulder, cut into small pieces
- 200g pork fatback, cut into small pieces
- 7g paprika
- 2 cloves of garlic, minced
- 15g salt
- 2g ground black pepper
- 2g dried oregano
- 2g ground cumin
- 2g ground coriander
- 2.5m hog casings

Instructions:

1. In a large bowl, combine the pork shoulder, pork fatback, paprika, minced garlic, salt, black pepper, dried oregano, ground cumin, and ground coriander. Mix well to evenly distribute the spices.

2. Cover the bowl with plastic wrap and refrigerate for 1-2 hours to allow the flavours to meld.

3. Rinse the hog casings under cold water and soak them according to the package instructions.

4. Attach a sausage stuffer nozzle to a sausage stuffer or a meat grinder with a sausage stuffing attachment.

5. Slide the soaked casing onto the nozzle, leaving a small overhang.

6. Stuff the sausage mixture into the casing, making sure to fill it evenly without air pockets. Guide the casing off the nozzle as you go.

7. Twist the sausage into links, about 10-12cm long, and tie off the ends.

8. Preheat your smoker to 110-120°C (225-250°F) using your preferred smoking wood chips or chunks.

9. Place the sausages on the smoker grates and smoke for 2-3 hours until they reach an internal temperature of 70°C (160°F).

10. Remove the sausages from the smoker and let them rest for a few minutes before serving.

11. Enjoy your homemade Smoked Chorizo Sausage! Serve it sliced as a tasty appetizer, use it in sandwiches, or incorporate it into various recipes for added flavour and spice.

SMOKED ITALIAN SAUSAGE

Ingredients:

- 800g pork shoulder, cut into small pieces
- 200g pork fatback, cut into small pieces
- 15g salt
- 5g fennel seeds
- 2g ground black pepper
- 2g paprika
- 2g dried parsley
- 2g dried basil
- 2g dried oregano
- 2.5m hog casings

Instructions:

1. In a large bowl, combine the pork shoulder, pork fatback, salt, fennel seeds, black pepper, paprika, dried parsley, dried basil, and dried oregano. Mix well to evenly distribute the spices.

2. Cover the bowl with plastic wrap and refrigerate for 1-2 hours to allow the flavours to meld.

3. Rinse the hog casings under cold water and soak them according to the package instructions.

4. Attach a sausage stuffer nozzle to a sausage stuffer or a meat grinder with a sausage stuffing attachment.

5. Slide the soaked casing onto the nozzle, leaving a small overhang.

6. Stuff the sausage mixture into the casing, making sure to fill it evenly without air pockets. Guide the casing off the nozzle as you go.

7. Twist the sausage into links, about 10-12cm long, and tie off the ends.

8. Preheat your smoker to 110-120°C (225-250°F) using your preferred smoking wood chips or chunks.

9. Place the sausages on the smoker grates and smoke for 2-3 hours until they reach an internal temperature of 70°C (160°F).

10. Remove the sausages from the smoker and let them rest for a few minutes before serving.

11. Enjoy your homemade Smoked Italian Sausage! Serve it grilled, sliced in sandwiches, or use it in various Italian recipes such as pasta sauces, pizzas, or soups.

SMOKED CAJUN SAUSAGE

Ingredients:

- 800g pork shoulder, cut into small pieces
- 200g pork fatback, cut into small pieces
- 15g salt
- 5g paprika
- 3g garlic powder
- 3g onion powder
- 2g dried thyme
- 2g dried oregano
- 2g dried basil
- 2g cayenne pepper
- 2g ground black pepper
- 2.5m hog casings

Instructions:

1. In a large bowl, combine the pork shoulder, pork fatback, salt, paprika, garlic powder, onion powder, dried thyme, dried oregano, dried basil, cayenne pepper, and ground black pepper. Mix well to evenly distribute the spices.

2. Cover the bowl with plastic wrap and refrigerate for 1-2 hours to allow the flavours to meld.

3. Rinse the hog casings under cold water and soak them according to the package instructions.

4. Attach a sausage stuffer nozzle to a sausage stuffer or a meat grinder with a sausage stuffing attachment.

5. Slide the soaked casing onto the nozzle, leaving a small overhang.

6. Stuff the sausage mixture into the casing, making sure to fill it evenly without air pockets. Guide the casing off the nozzle as you go.

7. Twist the sausage into links, about 10-12cm long, and tie off the ends.

8. Preheat your smoker to 110-120°C (225-250°F) using your preferred smoking wood chips or chunks.

9. Place the sausages on the smoker grates and smoke for 2-3 hours until they reach an internal temperature of 70°C (160°F).

10. Remove the sausages from the smoker and let them rest for a few minutes before serving.

11. Enjoy your homemade Smoked Cajun Sausage! Serve it grilled, sliced in sandwiches, or use it in various Cajun-inspired recipes such as jambalaya, gumbo, or po' boys.

SMOKED HOT LINK SAUSAGE

Ingredients:

- 1.4 kg venison
- 900 g fatty pork shoulder or belly
- 34 g salt (around 2 tbsp)
- 5 g Instacure no. 1 (optional, less than 1 tsp)
- 1 tbsp sugar (optional)
- 2 tbsp paprika
- 1 tbsp freshly ground black pepper
- 1 tbsp cayenne pepper
- 2 tsp thyme
- 6 bay leaves, ground finely
- 3 cloves garlic, minced
- 80 ml lager beer or ice water
- Hog casings

Instructions:

1. Cut the venison and pork into pieces that will fit into your grinder. Mix them well with the salt and sugar. Let it sit in the fridge for as long as possible, ideally overnight, to help the sausage bind.

2. Soak the hog casings in warm water, using about 3 to 4 meters.

3. Combine the spices and garlic with the meat and fat. Grind the mixture through a coarse die (around 10 mm) or the coarsest one you have. If the room temperature is above 21°C, grind into a container placed in ice to keep it cold.

4. If the meat is below 4°C, grind it again through a finer die (around 6 mm) or similar. If it's above 4°C, place it in the freezer for 30 minutes to cool down.

5. Add the beer (or water) to the meat mixture and mix well using your hands or a mixer with a paddle attachment set on low speed for about 2 minutes. The sausage should adhere and show whitish streaks.

6. Load the sausage mixture into a sausage stuffer.

7. Thread a casing onto the stuffer, leaving a few inches as a "tail" for tying later. Stuff the entire casing at once, leaving a tail at the other end. Repeat until all the sausage is stuffed.

8. Make links by pinching them off and twisting them in opposite directions to prevent unraveling. Alternatively, you can tie them with twine. Check out a video tutorial for link-making if needed. Tie off the ends of the casings.

9. Carefully compress the links to remove any air pockets and prick them with a needle if necessary, gently pressing the meat.

10. Hang the sausages at room temperature for an hour, or up to a day if the temperature is 4°C or below.

11. Smoke the hot links at around 93°C (200°F) until they reach an internal temperature of about 65°C (150°F). You can either enjoy them immediately or cool them by plunging into an ice water bath. Dry them off and store in the fridge for up to a week or freeze.

SMOKED LINGUICA (SMOKED PORTUGUESE SAUSAGE)

Ingredients:

- 225g fresh pork backfat
- 1 tbsp olive oil
- 7 cloves of garlic, minced
- 1.8kg pork butt, cut into 2.5cm chunks
- 240ml red table wine
- 240ml sweet paprika
- 80g powdered milk
- 45ml cider vinegar
- 45ml salt
- 30g white sugar
- 15ml hickory-flavored liquid smoke
- 30g dried marjoram
- 30g ground white pepper
- 15g ground black pepper
- 5g crushed red pepper
- a pinch of cayenne pepper
- 4 feet of hog casing
- Lump charcoal
- Hickory wood chunks
- Toothpicks

Instructions:

1. Rinse the pork backfat thoroughly and soak it in warm water for 30 minutes. Then chop it into small pieces.

2. Heat olive oil in a small pan and sauté the minced garlic for 30 seconds to 1 minute, ensuring it doesn't brown. Remove from the pan and transfer to a large bowl.

3. Add the chopped fatback, pork butt, red table wine, sweet paprika, powdered milk, cider vinegar, salt, sugar, liquid smoke, dried marjoram, ground white pepper, ground black pepper, crushed red pepper, and cayenne pepper to the bowl with the garlic. Mix everything well until thoroughly combined. Cover the bowl and refrigerate for 8 hours or overnight.

4. After marinating, test the sausage flavor by frying a small bit of it in a pan and tasting it. Adjust the spices if needed, and refrigerate the mixture for an additional 2 hours, covered.

5. Rinse the hog casings with water and soak them in warm water for 30 minutes.

6. Set up a sausage stuffing attachment on a KitchenAid⬚ or any other suitable sausage stuffer. Squeeze out water from a length of casing and tie one end in a knot. Slide the casing onto the sausage-making fitting.

7. Turn on the sausage stuffer to medium speed. Feed the cold sausage mixture into the funnel, using one hand to keep the casing tight and the other to feed the meat mixture. Twist off links as you reach the desired length. Repeat the process with the remaining hog casings and sausage mixture.

8. Prepare your smoker by adding several handfuls of hot charcoal to establish a base temperature, and then let the temperature drop to around 60°C (140°F). This ensures a cold smoke that doesn't cook the sausages or brown the skin.

9. Once the smoker reaches the desired temperature, add hickory wood chunks. The temperature will spike, so allow it to cool back down to 60°C (140°F).

10. Using toothpicks, hang the sausages in the smoker as far away from the direct heat source as possible. Maintain the temperature around 60°C (140°F) as best as you can, but don't worry if there are slight temperature fluctuations.

11. Smoke the sausages until they turn deep red and the skin starts to firm up, which should take about 1 ½ hours.

12. Remove the sausages from the smoker and let them rest for 30 minutes. Cook them like any other sausage before serving, either by pan-frying or grilling.

SMOKED GARLIC SAUSAGE

Ingredients:

- 1 kg fatty pork shoulder (Boston butt)
- 15 g kosher salt
- 2.5 g insta cure #1 (optional)
- 2 g white pepper
- 6 g mustard seed
- 1 g ginger powder
- 3.5 g garlic powder
- 12 cloves roasted garlic (or more, if desired)
- 20 g non-fat dry milk powder
- 60 ml ice-cold water
- Hog casings

Instructions:

1. Trim the pork shoulder, removing any silver skin, sinew, and arteries. Cut it into small strips or cubes.

2. Place the meat and fat in the freezer for about an hour or until the temperature reaches 0°C - 2°C.

3. Rehydrate and clean the hog casings according to the package instructions.

4. Grind the chilled meat mixture using a 6mm plate on your grinder.

5. In a bowl, combine the ground meat, salt, cure (if using), white pepper, mustard seed, ginger powder, garlic powder, roasted garlic, non-fat dry milk powder, and ice-cold water. Mix until the mixture becomes sticky and tacky.

6. Stuff the sausage mixture into the hog casings, forming links and ensuring there are no air pockets. Let the sausages rest in the refrigerator overnight.

7. Smoking Schedule:

   - Preheat your smoker to 38°C - 43°C and smoke the sausages for 1.5 hours with the door slightly ajar or vents open to dry them.

   - Close the door and increase the temperature to 52°C. Add your favorite wood chips for smoke.

   - Smoke at 57°C for 1 hour, then increase the temperature to 68°C for 1.5 hours.

   - Finally, raise the temperature to 79°C until the internal temperature of the sausages reaches 63°C.

8. After smoking, cool the sausages in ice water and let them bloom at room temperature for several hours.

9. Cover the sausages and refrigerate overnight. They can be stored in the refrigerator for up to 1 week or frozen in vacuum-sealed bags for 9+ months.

SMOKED CHEESE SAUSAGE

Ingredients:

- Ingredients:
-
- 10 feet (32-35mm) natural hog casings
- 1.81 kg boneless pork shoulder, diced into 1/2 inch cubes
- 453.59 g pork back fat, cubed
- 2 1/2 tablespoons kosher salt
- 1 teaspoon Prague powder #1 (optional)
- 1 tablespoon sweet paprika powder

- 1 tablespoon freshly ground black pepper
- 1 teaspoon dried thyme
- 1 teaspoon garlic powder
- 1 teaspoon onion powder
- 2 teaspoons dry ground mustard
- 122.5 g non-fat dry milk
- 118.29 ml ice water
- 453.59 g cheddar cheese, diced into 1/8 inch cubes

- **Instructions:**

1. Freeze the diced pork for 45 minutes until it reaches 0°C (32°F).
2. Grind the pork and fat using a 6mm (1/4 inch) plate. Grind it twice, keeping the meat cold by placing the bowl on ice.
3. Combine all the spices in a small bowl.
4. In a stand mixer, mix the ground meat, spice mix, dry milk, and ice water for 3-4 minutes until threads appear.
5. Stir in the diced cheddar cheese and chill the mixture in the refrigerator.
6. Optional: Taste a small portion of the mixture and adjust the seasonings if needed.
7. Thread the hog casings onto the sausage stuffer.
8. Fill the casings with the meat mixture, avoiding air gaps and overstuffing.
9. Twist the sausages into 6-inch links and prick any air bubbles.
10. Chill the sausages overnight.
11. Preheat the smoker to 79-85°C (175-185°F) and smoke the sausages until the internal temperature reaches 71°C (160°F).
12. Cool the sausages quickly by spraying them with cold water.
13. Allow the sausages to air dry for 1-2 hours.
14. Store the sausages in the refrigerator for 3-4 days or freeze them for up to 3 months.
15. Reheat the sausages by pan frying or grilling.
16. This recipe yields approximately 24 sausages, depending on the casing size and stuffing density.

SMOKED VENISON SAUSAGE

Ingredients:

- 1.36 kg venison or other wild game meat
- 1.36 kg fatty pork belly or trims
- 113.4 g Butter Garlic Brat Seasoning
- 85 g Binder Flour
- 1 1/4 teaspoons Pink Cure
- 120 ml water
- Natural Hog Casings (32-35 mm)

Instructions:

1. Cut the venison and pork belly into small pieces. Place them in the freezer for 15-20 minutes.

2. Set up the grinder with a 3/8" plate. Grind the meat through the grinder once.

3. Mix the Butter Garlic Brat Seasoning with the ground meat. Chill the mixture.

4. Change the grinder plate to a 3/16" plate and grind the seasoned meat again.

5. Add the binder flour and pink cure to the meat mixture. Mix well using your hands or a meat mixer.

6. Add water to the mixture and mix until the meat sticks together.

7. Prepare the sausage stuffer with a 3/4" horn. Load the stuffer with the meat mixture, making sure there are no air pockets.

8. Thread the natural hog casings onto the horn. Stuff the meat mixture into the casings, leaving space to twist them into links.

9. Twist the sausages into links and remove any air pockets using a sausage pricker or a sharp knife.

10. Place the sausages on a tray lined with a rack. Refrigerate overnight to allow them to dry and develop flavors.

11. Preheat the smoker to 130 degrees F (54 degrees Celsius). Hang the sausages in the smoker with space between them. Smoke for 30 minutes.

12. Add moistened sawdust to the smoker and increase the temperature to 150 degrees F (65 degrees Celsius). Smoke for 45 minutes.

13. Remove the sawdust and increase the temperature to 170 degrees F (77 degrees Celsius). Cook the sausages for 2-3 hours until the internal temperature reaches 155 degrees F (68 degrees Celsius).

14. Transfer the sausages to an ice bath for 15-20 minutes to cool quickly.

15. Store the sausages in vacuum-sealed bags for future use or grill them immediately and enjoy!

16. Optional: Add high-temp cheese or crushed jalapenos for extra flavor.

SMOKED CHICKEN SAUSAGE

Ingredients:

- 2.2 lbs (1 kg) chicken meat with skins and fat
- 2 tsp + a small pinch (13 g) kosher salt
- A touch less than 1/2 tsp (2.14 g) Cure #1
- 2 tbsp (12 g) Fermento
- 2/3 tsp (2.5 g) sugar
- 2/3 tsp (2 g) granulated garlic
- 3/4 tsp (1.5 g) coarsely ground black pepper
- 2 tsp (1.5 g) rubbed sage
- 2 tsp (1 g) dried parsley
- 1/4 tsp (0.5 g) ground nutmeg
- Optional: 1/4 tsp (0.5 g) cayenne pepper
- 1/4 cup (60 ml) chilled chicken broth or ice water

Instructions:

1. Cut the chicken meat into 2-inch (5-6 cm) pieces and mix it with salt and Cure #1. Place it in a container, cover, and refrigerate for 24-48 hours (optional step).

2. Grind the meat with skins and fat using a 1/8-inch (3 mm) plate.

3. Mix the ground meat with Fermento, sugar, granulated garlic, black pepper, rubbed sage, dried parsley, nutmeg, and cayenne pepper (if using). Add the chilled chicken broth or ice water.

4. Stuff the mixture firmly into sheep or young hog casings, making about 12-inch links and tying them with butcher's twine. Prick any air pockets with a clean needle.

5. Dry the sausages in a cold room or refrigerator at 35-43°F (2-6°C) for 12 hours or at room temperature for about 60 minutes. Alternatively, you can dry them in a smoker at 110-130°F (43-54°C) without smoke for about 30 minutes until the casings feel dry to the touch.

6. Smoke the sausages at 130-140°F (54-60°C) for 1 hour until the casings turn dark brown. Then, increase the smoker temperature gradually to 165°F (74°C), 175°F (79°C), 185°F (85°C), and even 195°F (90°C) if necessary, until the internal temperature of the sausages reaches 160°F (71°C).

7. Alternatively, you can poach the sausages in water at 167-172°F (75-78°C) for 15-20 minutes until the internal temperature reaches 160°F (71°C).

8. If desired, you can further dry the sausages at 53-64°F (12-18°C) and 75-80% relative humidity for 5-7 days until there is a 45% total weight loss.

9. Store the sausages in the refrigerator, whether dried or undried.

   Note: It's recommended to use a precision scale and measure the ingredients in grams for better accuracy. To adapt the recipe to different quantities, calculate the multiplier for each ingredient by dividing the weight of your chicken meat by 1000 and multiplying it by the original amount.

SMOKED BEEF SAUSAGE

Ingredients:

- 5 lbs (2.3 kg) Certified Angus Beef chuck (or something similar)
- 2 tbsp kosher salt
- 2 tsp dehydrated minced garlic
- 2 tsp dried marjoram
- 2 tsp coarsely ground black pepper
- 2 tsp sugar
- 1 tsp ground ancho chile powder
- 1 tsp smoked paprika
- 1 tsp pink curing salt #1
- 3/4 cup ice water
- Natural pork casings

Instructions:

1. Cut the beef into cubes.

2. Set up the meat grinder with a larger die and grind the meat into a bowl.

3. Mix in the spices and water by hand, then place the mixture in the freezer for at least 10 minutes.

4. Change to a smaller die on the meat grinder and pass the meat through it again.

5. Cook a small patty to taste and adjust the seasoning if needed.

6. Cover the bowl and refrigerate the meat for 24 hours.

7. Pack the meat into a sausage stuffer and slide the casings onto the tube.

8. Place the links on a sheet pan lined with a rack and refrigerate uncovered for another 24 hours.

9. Preheat the smoker to 160°F (71°C) and smoke the sausages for 1 hour.

10. Increase the temperature to 170°F (77°C) and smoke for 1 hour.

11. Increase the temperature to 180°F (82°C) and continue smoking until the internal temperature of the sausages reaches 160°F (71°C), which takes about 3 hours.

12. Remove the sausages from the smoker and place them in an ice water bath until the internal temperature reaches 120°F (49°C).

13. Transfer the sausages to a sheet pan lined with a rack and let them cool to room temperature.

14. Refrigerate the sausages for up to one week or freeze them for up to 9 months.

15. Note: Keep the meat cold throughout the process to ensure food safety.

SMOKED TURKEY SAUSAGE

Ingredients:

- 800g pork shoulder, cut into small pieces
- 200g pork fatback, cut into small pieces
- 15g salt
- 5g paprika
- 3g garlic powder
- 3g onion powder
- 2g dried thyme
- 2g dried oregano
- 2g dried basil
- 2g cayenne pepper
- 2g ground black pepper
- 2.5m hog casings

Instructions:

1. In a large bowl, combine the pork shoulder, pork fatback, salt, paprika, garlic powder, onion powder, dried thyme, dried oregano, dried basil, cayenne pepper, and ground black pepper. Mix well to evenly distribute the spices.

2. Cover the bowl with plastic wrap and refrigerate for 1-2 hours to allow the flavours to meld.

3. Rinse the hog casings under cold water and soak them according to the package instructions.

4. Attach a sausage stuffer nozzle to a sausage stuffer or a meat grinder with a sausage stuffing attachment.

5. Slide the soaked casing onto the nozzle, leaving a small overhang.

6. Stuff the sausage mixture into the casing, making sure to fill it evenly without air pockets. Guide the casing off the nozzle as you go.

7. Twist the sausage into links, about 10-12cm long, and tie off the ends.

8. Preheat your smoker to 110-120°C (225-250°F) using your preferred smoking wood chips or chunks.

9. Place the sausages on the smoker grates and smoke for 2-3 hours until they reach an internal temperature of 70°C (160°F).

10. Remove the sausages from the smoker and let them rest for a few minutes before serving.

11. Enjoy your homemade Smoked Cajun Sausage! Serve it grilled, sliced in sandwiches, or use it in various Cajun-inspired recipes such as jambalaya, gumbo, or po' boys.

SMOKED LAMB SAUSAGE

Ingredients:

- 5 tbsp olive oil
- 5 garlic cloves
- 5 lbs lamb shoulder
- 2 lbs pork fat
- 2 tbsp paprika
- 2 tbsp cayenne
- 2 tbsp cumin seeds
- 2 tbsp chili powder
- 5 tbsp kosher salt
- 2 ½ tsp sugar

Instructions:

1. Preheat the smoker to 230°F (110°C) and soak wood chips for an hour.

2. Sauté garlic in olive oil until fragrant.

3. Toast cumin seeds in a dry skillet, then grind them.

4. Cube lamb shoulder into 1-inch pieces.

5. In a bowl, mix lamb shoulder, pork fat, sautéed garlic, ground cumin seeds, paprika, cayenne, chili powder, kosher salt, and sugar.

6. Cover and refrigerate the mixture for 24 hours.

7. Grind the marinated mixture through a meat grinder twice.

8. Rinse the casings with water.

9. Attach a casing to the sausage stuffer and fill with the ground mixture.

10. Stuff the mixture into the casings, twisting to form links.

11. Preheat the smoker, place wood chips in the chip box.

12. Hang the sausages on hooks or place on racks in the smoker.

13. Smoke at 220°F (105°C) for about 1 hour.

14. Check the internal temperature of the sausages with a meat thermometer, aiming for 140°F (60°C).

15. Serve the lamb sausages with Greek yogurt or tzatziki.

SMOKED ELK POLISH KIELBASA SAUSAGE

Ingredients:

- Meat: 2.78 to 4.0 pounds (depending on desired fat content)
- Fat: 1.0 to 2.22 pounds (depending on fat content)
- Kosher salt: 2 tablespoons
- Ground black pepper: 2 teaspoons
- Marjoram: 2-3 teaspoons
- Garlic cloves: 3-6 (minced or crushed)

- Prague Powder #1: 1 teaspoon (for 5 lbs of meat)
- Ice water: 3/4 cup
- Sausage casings (hog, sheep, or collagen)

Optional Ingredients:

- Sugar: 2 1/4 tablespoons
- Dry Mustard: 2 1/4 tablespoons
- Ground red pepper: 2 teaspoons

Instructions:

1. In a large bowl, combine the pork shoulder, pork fatback, salt, paprika, garlic powder, onion powder, dried thyme, dried oregano, dried basil, cayenne pepper, and ground black pepper. Mix well to evenly distribute the spices.

2. Cover the bowl with plastic wrap and refrigerate for 1-2 hours to allow the flavours to meld.

3. Rinse the hog casings under cold water and soak them according to the package instructions.

4. Attach a sausage stuffer nozzle to a sausage stuffer or a meat grinder with a sausage stuffing attachment.

5. Slide the soaked casing onto the nozzle, leaving a small overhang.

6. Stuff the sausage mixture into the casing, making sure to fill it evenly without air pockets. Guide the casing off the nozzle as you go.

7. Twist the sausage into links, about 10-12cm long, and tie off the ends.

8. Preheat your smoker to 110-120°C (225-250°F) using your preferred smoking wood chips or chunks.

9. Place the sausages on the smoker grates and smoke for 2-3 hours until they reach an internal temperature of 70°C (160°F).

10. Remove the sausages from the smoker and let them rest for a few minutes before serving.

11. Enjoy your homemade Smoked Cajun Sausage! Serve it grilled, sliced in sandwiches, or use it in various Cajun-inspired recipes such as jambalaya, gumbo, or po' boys.

SMOKED BISON SAUSAGE

Ingredients:

- 2 pounds bison meat
- 1/2 pound pork fat
- 2 tablespoons kosher salt
- 2 teaspoons black pepper
- 1 teaspoon garlic powder
- 1 teaspoon onion powder
- 1 teaspoon dried thyme
- 1 teaspoon smoked paprika
- 1/2 teaspoon dried sage
- 1/2 teaspoon dried rosemary
- 1/4 teaspoon cayenne pepper
- 1/4 cup ice water
- Sausage casings (hog, sheep, or collagen)

Instructions:

1. Ensure the bison meat and pork fat are chilled. Cut them into small pieces for grinding.

2. Using a meat grinder, grind the bison meat and pork fat together.

3. In a mixing bowl, combine the ground meat and fat with all the spices and the ice water. Mix well until the ingredients are evenly distributed.

4. Prepare the sausage casings by rinsing them under water and removing any excess salt.

5. Attach a sausage stuffer to the grinder and load the mixture into the stuffer.

6. Slide the casings onto the sausage stuffer's tube, leaving a few inches of casing empty at the end.

7. Begin stuffing the mixture into the casings, guiding it with your hands. Fill the casings evenly, leaving some space between each sausage.

8. Once all the mixture is used and the sausages are stuffed, twist or tie off the casings to create individual links.

9. Preheat your smoker to 225°F (107°C) and prepare it with your choice of wood chips for smoking flavor.

10. Place the sausages on the smoker racks, leaving some space between them for even smoking.

11. Smoke the sausages at 225°F (107°C) for approximately 2-3 hours or until they reach an internal temperature of 160°F (71°C).

12. Once smoked, remove the sausages from the smoker and let them cool for a few minutes.

13. Serve the smoked bison sausages hot and enjoy their delicious flavor.

SMOKED WILD BOAR SAUSAGE

Ingredients:

- 2 pounds wild boar meat
- 1/2 pound pork fat
- 2 tablespoons kosher salt
- 2 teaspoons black pepper
- 1 teaspoon garlic powder
- 1 teaspoon onion powder
- 1 teaspoon dried thyme
- 1 teaspoon smoked paprika
- 1/2 teaspoon dried sage
- 1/2 teaspoon dried rosemary
- 1/4 teaspoon cayenne pepper
- 1/4 cup ice water
- Sausage casings (hog, sheep, or collagen)

Instructions:

1. Ensure the wild boar meat and pork fat are chilled. Cut them into small pieces for grinding.

2. Using a meat grinder, grind the wild boar meat and pork fat together.

3. In a mixing bowl, combine the ground meat and fat with all the spices and the ice water. Mix well until the ingredients are evenly distributed.

4. Prepare the sausage casings by rinsing them under water and removing any excess salt.

5. Attach a sausage stuffer to the grinder and load the mixture into the stuffer.

6. Slide the casings onto the sausage stuffer's tube, leaving a few inches of casing empty at the end.

7. Begin stuffing the mixture into the casings, guiding it with your hands. Fill the casings evenly, leaving some space between each sausage.

8. Once all the mixture is used and the sausages are stuffed, twist or tie off the casings to create individual links.

9. Preheat your smoker to 225°F (107°C) and prepare it with your choice of wood chips for smoking flavor.

10. Place the sausages on the smoker racks, leaving some space between them for even smoking.

11. Smoke the sausages at 225°F (107°C) for approximately 2-3 hours or until they reach an internal temperature of 160°F (71°C).

12. Once smoked, remove the sausages from the smoker and let them cool for a few minutes.

13. Serve the smoked wild boar sausages hot and enjoy their rich and gamey flavor.

SMOKED GAME SAUSAGE

Ingredients:

- 2 pounds mixed game meat (such as venison, elk, or wild boar)
- 1/2 pound pork fat
- 2 tablespoons kosher salt
- 2 teaspoons black pepper
- 1 teaspoon garlic powder
- 1 teaspoon onion powder
- 1 teaspoon dried thyme
- 1 teaspoon smoked paprika
- 1/2 teaspoon dried sage
- 1/2 teaspoon dried rosemary
- 1/4 teaspoon cayenne pepper
- 1/4 cup ice water
- Sausage casings (hog, sheep, or collagen)

Instructions:

1. Ensure the game meat and pork fat are chilled. Cut them into small pieces for grinding.

2. Using a meat grinder, grind the game meat and pork fat together.

3. In a mixing bowl, combine the ground meat and fat with all the spices and the ice water. Mix well until the ingredients are evenly distributed.

4. Prepare the sausage casings by rinsing them under water and removing any excess salt.

5. Attach a sausage stuffer to the grinder and load the mixture into the stuffer.

6. Slide the casings onto the sausage stuffer's tube, leaving a few inches of casing empty at the end.

7. Begin stuffing the mixture into the casings, guiding it with your hands. Fill the casings evenly, leaving some space between each sausage.

8. Once all the mixture is used and the sausages are stuffed, twist or tie off the casings to create individual links.

9. Preheat your smoker to 225°F (107°C) and prepare it with your choice of wood chips for smoking flavor.

10. Place the sausages on the smoker racks, leaving some space between them for even smoking.

11. Smoke the sausages at 225°F (107°C) for approximately 2-3 hours or until they reach an internal temperature of 160°F (71°C).

12. Once smoked, remove the sausages from the smoker and let them cool for a few minutes.

13. Serve the smoked game sausages hot and enjoy the unique and flavorful taste of the wild game.

SMOKED SEAFOOD SAUSAGE

Ingredients:

- 1.76 lbs (800 g) fish (sea bass or any fish of choice)
- 0.44 lbs (200 g) pork backfat
- 2.5 tsp kosher salt
- 1/2 tsp Insta Cure #1 (curing salt)
- 1/2 tsp white pepper
- 1/2 tsp dried marjoram
- 1 tsp minced garlic
- 0.71 oz (20 g) potato starch
- 1.5 tsp lime zest
- 1/4 cup (60 ml) very cold cream (or any preferred liquid)
- 1 egg (optional, for binding and texture)
- Hog casings

Instructions:

1. Clean the fish and fat, then cut them into small strips or cubes. Place in the freezer until the temperature reaches 32°F (0°C).

2. Grind the chilled fish and fat using a medium plate (6mm).

3. Prepare all the seasonings and liquids. Add them to the chilled meat and mix until the mixture becomes tacky (avoid overworking).

4. Stuff the mixture into hog casings, linking the sausages and pricking out any air pockets. Let them rest in the refrigerator overnight.

5. The next day, smoke the sausages using incremental temperature adjustments to slowly reach a core temperature of 145°F (62.7°C). Apple wood or pecan wood is recommended for smoking white fish.

6. If using a digital smoker:

- 1.5 hours at 100°F (37.7°C) to dry the sausage (leave dampers wide open)
- 1.5 hours at 125°F (51.6°C) while applying smoke
- 1 hour at 155°F (68.3°C)
- 1 hour at 175°F (79.4°C)
- Increase to 200°F (93.3°C) until the internal temperature reaches 145°F (62.7°C)

7. If using a pit or offset smoker:

- Start smoking sausages on indirect heat at 150°F (65.5°C) for 3 hours.
- Increase the temperature to 200°F (93.3°C) and cook until the internal temperature reaches 145°F (62.7°C).

SMOKED VEGETARIAN SAUSAGE

Ingredients:

- 1.76 lb (800 g) wheat gluten
- 3.5 oz (100 g) soy emulsion
- 1.76 oz (50 g) vital wheat gluten
- 0.7 oz (20 g) potato starch
- 0.35 oz (10 g) guar gum
- 0.35 oz (10 g) carrageenan
- 0.35 oz (10 g) salt
- 0.14 oz (4 g) pepper
- 0.03 oz (1 g) marjoram
- 0.17 oz (5 g) garlic powder
- 0.5 fl oz (15 ml) liquid smoke

Instructions:

1. Grind the wheat gluten using a 3/8" (10 mm) plate.

2. In a mixing bowl, combine the ground gluten with soy emulsion and spices.

3. Add vital wheat gluten, potato starch, guar gum, and carrageenan to the mixture. Mix everything together until well combined.

4. Stuff the mixture tightly into 38 mm casings.

5. Cook the sausages in water maintained at 176-185°F (80-85°C) for 20 minutes.

6. Transfer the cooked sausages to cold water and let them soak for 5 minutes.

7. Remove the sausages from the water and allow them to cool.

Note:

To make the soy emulsion, use the given ratio (by weight) of soy protein isolate, vegetable oil, and water. Mix the soy protein isolate with water until a smooth paste is obtained, then gradually add oil until a mayonnaise-like emulsion is achieved. 100 g of soy protein emulsion is made from 10 g soy protein isolate, 40 g oil, and 50 g water.

SMOKED PLANT-BASED SAUSAGE

Ingredients:

- 2 cups vital wheat gluten
- 1/4 cup nutritional yeast
- 2 tablespoons paprika
- 2 tablespoons garlic powder
- 1 tablespoon onion powder
- 1 tablespoon fennel seeds
- 1 tablespoon dried oregano
- 1 teaspoon smoked paprika
- 1 teaspoon black pepper
- 1 teaspoon salt
- 1 1/2 cups vegetable broth
- 1/4 cup soy sauce
- 2 tablespoons tomato paste
- 2 tablespoons liquid smoke

Instructions:

1. In a large mixing bowl, combine the vital wheat gluten, nutritional yeast, paprika, garlic powder, onion powder, fennel seeds, dried oregano, smoked paprika, black pepper, and salt. Mix well to evenly distribute the dry ingredients.

2. In a separate bowl, whisk together the vegetable broth, soy sauce, tomato paste, and liquid smoke.

3. Pour the liquid mixture into the dry ingredients. Stir until a dough forms.

4. Knead the dough for about 5 minutes to develop the gluten.

5. Divide the dough into equal-sized portions and shape each portion into a sausage shape.

6. Preheat your smoker to 225°F (107°C).

7. Place the sausages on a smoking rack and transfer them to the preheated smoker.

8. Smoke the sausages for about 2 hours, or until they develop a smoky flavor and firm texture.

9. Remove the sausages from the smoker and let them cool before serving or storing.

HOT-SMOKED SAUSAGE (HONEY GARLIC)

Ingredients:

- 5 lbs pork butt
- 1 1/2 tbsp kosher salt
- 1 tsp Cure #1 (optional)
- 1 1/3 tsp white pepper (heaping)
- 3 large cloves garlic, pressed
- 2 tbsp honey
- 1 cup ice water

Instructions:

1. Cut the pork butt into 2" pieces. If using Cure #1, mix it with the salt.

2. Grind the pork using a small size plate (1/8" or 3mm).

3. Add the ice water, honey, garlic, and white pepper to the ground pork. Mix well until the meat becomes sticky.

4. Stuff the mixture into 28-32mm hog casings, twisting them into 6-7" links. Cut into individual links.

5. Preheat your smoker to 225°F using indirect heat.

6. Place the sausages in the smoker and smoke them until they reach an internal temperature of 160°F, which should take around 1.5 hours.

7. Cool the sausages quickly by placing them in a Ziploc bag in an ice bath. This helps retain their plumpness and texture.

8. Store the sausages wrapped in butcher's paper in the refrigerator, or vacuum seal and freeze them.

9. For improved texture, flavor intensity, and shelf life, you can dry the sausages in a cold room or curing chamber at 55°F and 75% relative humidity (RH).

PORK AND MUSTARD SMOKED SAUSAGE

Ingredients:

- 2 cups vital wheat gluten
- 1/4 cup nutritional yeast
- 2 tablespoons paprika
- 2 tablespoons garlic powder
- 1 tablespoon onion powder
- 1 tablespoon fennel seeds
- 1 tablespoon dried oregano
- 1 teaspoon smoked paprika
- 1 teaspoon black pepper
- 1 teaspoon salt
- 1 1/2 cups vegetable broth
- 1/4 cup soy sauce
- 2 tablespoons tomato paste
- 2 tablespoons liquid smoke

Instructions:

1. In a large bowl, combine the ground pork, ground mustard, onion powder, garlic powder, pink curing salt, kosher salt, and black pepper. Mix well to evenly distribute the seasonings.

2. Add the ice water to the mixture and continue mixing until the ingredients are thoroughly combined and the mixture becomes sticky.

3. Prepare the hog casings by soaking them in cold water according to the package instructions. Rinse them under cold water to remove any excess salt.

4. Attach the sausage stuffer to a sausage-making machine or use a sausage stuffer attachment for a stand mixer.

5. Slide one end of a soaked hog casing onto the sausage stuffer nozzle, leaving a few inches hanging off the end. Push the casing onto the nozzle, allowing it to coil up.

6. Stuff the sausage mixture into the casings, twisting the sausages at regular intervals to form individual links. Leave some extra casing at the end to tie off the sausages.

7. Once all the sausages are stuffed, refrigerate them for at least 1 hour to allow the flavors to meld and the sausages to firm up.

8. You can now cook the sausages according to your preference, whether grilling, pan-frying, or baking them.

9. Enjoy your homemade sausages!

DRY CURED SAUSAGES

SPANISH CHORIZO SAUSAGES

Ingredients:

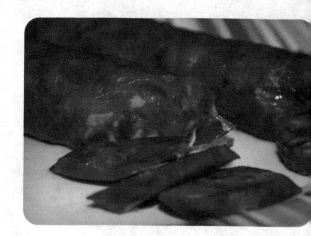

- 800g pork (e.g., pork shoulder)
- 200g pork fat (e.g., fatback, skin removed)
- 7g spicy paprika (pimentón de la Vera)
- 14g sweet paprika (pimentón de la Vera)
- 2 cloves garlic
- 17g salt
- 2.5g curing salt (optional, for dry-cured variety)
- Dash of white wine (optional)
- 2.5m pork casings

Instructions:

1. Grind the pork and pork fat using a meat grinder, ensuring the fat is slightly frozen to maintain texture.
2. In a mixing bowl, combine the ground meat, spicy paprika, sweet paprika, garlic, salt, and optional curing salt. Gently mix the ingredients until evenly dispersed, avoiding overmixing.
3. Cover the mixture with plastic wrap and refrigerate overnight to allow the flavors to meld together.
4. If using salted pork casings, soak them in water for about an hour (according to packaging instructions), and rinse them thoroughly.
5. Slide the casings onto the nozzle of a sausage stuffer.
6. Slowly and carefully fill the casings with the sausage mixture, using a sausage stuffer or an alternative tool like an electric cookie press.
7. Tie off the ends of each sausage with a small knot, and cut off any excess casing. Check for air gaps and prick the casing with a sterilized needle to release trapped air.
8. For fresh chorizo, you can pan-fry or grill the sausages until fully cooked.
9. To dry-cure the chorizo, tie a cotton cord around the ends and hang it in a cool, dry place for several weeks. Monitor the weight loss (approximately 35%) for desired texture.
10. Once cured, slice the homemade Spanish chorizo and enjoy it with or without the casing.

Notes: Use high-quality pork and fresh ingredients for the best results.
Keep the meat mixture and equipment cold throughout the process to maintain texture and prevent fat from melting.
Adjust the amount of paprika and seasoning to suit your taste preference.
Conduct a seasoning test by cooking a small portion of the mixture before stuffing the sausages.
If possible, invest in a dedicated sausage stuffer for easier and more even stuffing.
Ensure casings are fully rinsed to remove excess salt.
Store leftover chorizo in airtight containers or freezer bags, refrigerating or freezing as needed. For dry-cure follow the step 9.

Italian Salami

Ingredients:

- 500g lean pork
- 250g lean beef
- 250g pork back fat
- 27.5g kosher salt
- 2g dextrose
- 4g table sugar
- 4g black pepper
- 20g minced garlic
- 7g fennel seeds
- 75ml red wine
- Rehydrated mold 600 (1/2 tsp of mold in 1/2 cup of non-chlorinated water)
- Hog casings (32-34mm)

Instructions:

1. If using mold culture, prepare it at least 2-3 hours before needed to activate it.

2. Soak the hog casings in water to prepare them for stuffing.

3. Clean and sanitize all your equipment and tools for a hygienic process.

4. Combine the red wine and minced garlic, and let them marinate for a few hours.

5. Trim the meat of any sinew or silverskin and cut the pork, beef, and pork back fat into small chunks that fit into your grinder.

6. Chill the meat and fat to below 34°F (1.1°C). Grind the chilled meat and fat using a 6mm plate. Rechill the ground meat.

7. Once the meat is rechilled, add all the spices, wine with garlic, and mix thoroughly until everything is well incorporated. The mixture should feel tacky and stick to your hand when turned upside down.

8. Stuff the mixture into the hog casings, pricking them with a sausage pricker. If using mold, brush it onto the surface of the salami. Weigh the salami and record the weight.

9. Ferment the salami by placing it in an environment with a temperature between 65°F (18°C) and 80°F (26.6°C) and high humidity for 24-48 hours. If it's cooler, ferment for 48 hours; if it's warmer, ferment for 24 hours. You can achieve high humidity by wrapping the salami in cling film or placing it in a large zip lock bag to retain moisture.

10. Once fermentation is complete, start the drying process. Set the drying conditions to 55°F (13°C) and 80% humidity. Leave the salami in these conditions until it loses 40% of its initial weight. The more moisture lost, the firmer the salami will be. Aim for a weight loss of 35% to 40%.

11. After reaching the desired weight loss, the salami is ready. Slice it thinly and enjoy!

HUNGARIAN CSABAI

Ingredients:

- Meat (1 kg):
- Salt: 28 g (3 tsp)
- Cure #2: 2.5 g (1/2 tsp)
- Pepper: 2.0 g (1 tsp)
- Sweet Paprika: 9.0 g (3 tsp)
- Hot Paprika: 9.0 g (3 tsp)
- Crushed Caraway Seeds: 3.0 g (1-1/2 tsp)
- Garlic, smashed: 7.0 g (2 cloves)

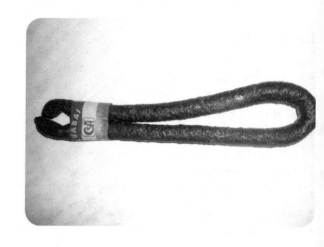

Instructions:

1. Remove sinews, gristle, and connective tissue from the meat manually.

2. Grind the meat using a 1/4" (6 mm) plate.

3. Grind the fat using a 1/4" (6 mm) plate.

4. In a mixing bowl, combine the ground meat, salt, cure #2, and spices. Mix well.

5. Stuff the mixture into 40-60 mm hog or synthetic fibrous casings, forming 8-22" (20-55 cm) links.

6. Apply a thin cold smoke for 3-5 days at 20°C (66°F), with 70-90% humidity. Use beech wood for an authentic Gyulai kolbasz flavor.

7. Dry the sausages for 4-6 weeks at 18°C - 16°C (64-60°F), with 90-92% humidity. Gradually reduce humidity to 70% - 65%.

8. Store the sausages at 12°C (54°F) with 65% humidity.

FRENCH SAUCISSON SEC

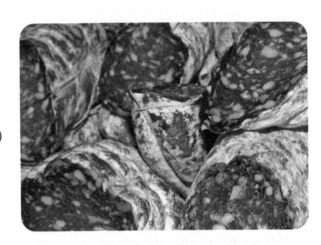

Ingredients:

- Pork meat: 4 1/2 pounds (2 kilograms)
- Fatback: 1/2 pound (225 grams)
- Kosher salt: 1 1/2 ounces (40 grams)
- Coarsely ground black pepper: 1/4 to 1/2 ounce (10 grams)
- Dextrose: 1/2 ounce (15 grams)
- Curing salt no. 2: 1/4 ounce (6 grams)
- Garlic, minced to a paste: 2/3 ounce (18 grams)
- Dry white wine: 1/4 cup (59 milliliters)
- Hog casing or sheep casing: 8 feet,
  soaked in tepid water for 2 hours before use

Instructions:

1. Set up a meat grinder and grind the pork meat and fatback using a large plate (3/4 inch/1.9 cm). Place the ground meat in a mixing bowl.

2. Add the kosher salt, black pepper, dextrose, curing salt no. 2, minced garlic, and dry white wine to the bowl. Mix well using a paddle or spoon.

3. Keep the casing wet in a bowl of water while working with it. Slide the casing onto the funnel of the stuffer without making a knot. Pack the meat mixture into the stuffer.

4. Begin extruding the sausage mixture. As it comes out, pull the casing back over the nozzle and tie a knot.

5. Extrude the mixture to form a full coil, approximately 48 inches (1.3 m) long, and tie it off.

6. Crimp with your fingers to separate the sausages into 12-inch (30 cm) lengths. Twist the casing once in one direction, then in the other between each sausage link. Repeat this along the entire coil.

7. Once the sausages are cased, use a sterile needle to prick any air pockets. Prick each sausage 4 or 5 times. Repeat the casing process to use the remaining sausage.

8. Hang the sausages to cure for 18 to 20 days at a temperature between 60°F and 75°F (15.5°C and 24°C).

9. Once cured, the sausages can be refrigerated, wrapped, for up to 6 months.

GERMAN METTWURST

Ingredients:

- 3 lbs (1.4 kg) pork shoulder
- 1 lb (450 g) veal
- 1 lb (450 g) lean beef chuck
- 2 tablespoons kosher salt
- 1 tablespoon ground white pepper
- 1 teaspoon ground coriander
- 1 teaspoon ground celery seed
- 1 teaspoon allspice
- 1/2 teaspoon ground dried marjoram
- 1/2 teaspoon ground caraway seed
- 1 teaspoon whole mustard seed
- 1 level teaspoon Instacure or Prague powder #1

Instructions:

1. Trim the pork, veal, and beef. Cut them into 1-inch cubes and refrigerate for 30 minutes to chill.

2. Grind the meat through the medium or fine plate of your meat grinder.

3. In a separate bowl, combine the kosher salt, white pepper, coriander, celery seed, allspice, dried marjoram, caraway seed, mustard seed, and Instacure or Prague powder #1. Mix them thoroughly.

4. Add the spice mixture to the ground meat and mix for at least 2 minutes, ensuring even distribution. Use your hands for mixing.

5. Once the sausage is fully mixed, grind it once more through the fine plate of your meat grinder.

6. Stuff the finely ground sausage into casings, using large pork casings or small beef rounds for best results.

7. Prepare the sausage for smoking in a meat smoker.

8. Smoke the sausage with a heavy smudge at 100-120°F (38-49°C) for at least 6 hours. Then, increase the smoker temperature to 160°F (71°C) and continue cooking until the internal temperature reaches 152°F (67°C).

9. Shower the sausage with water to cool it down and bloom for several hours.

10. After blooming, refrigerate the sausage overnight before packaging.

POLISH KABANOSY

Ingredients:

- 2 1/2 pounds (1.1 kg) pork venison, wild boar, bear, or other meat
- 10 ounces (280 g) pork fat
- 2 tablespoons plus 1 teaspoon (23 grams) kosher salt
- 1/4 teaspoon (3 grams) Instacure No. 1
- 1 heaping teaspoon (4 grams) sugar
- 2 teaspoons (4 grams) crushed black pepper
- 1 heaping teaspoon (2 grams) nutmeg
- 2 teaspoons (2 grams) caraway seed
- 1/4 teaspoon (1 gram) celery seed
- 4 cloves garlic, minced
- 1/3 cup (80 ml) ice water
- 20 feet sheep casings, soaked in tepid water

Instructions:

1. Cut the meat and fat into pieces that fit your grinder. Mix all the salts and spices with the meat and fat. Place everything in the freezer for 1 hour to chill. Meanwhile, soak the sheep casings in tepid water.

2. Grind the mixture using the fine die of your grinder, ensuring everything stays cold. If the meat warms beyond 35°F (2°C), freeze everything for 30 minutes to cool it down. Place the ground meat in the fridge while you clean up.

3. Using a stand mixer or your clean hands, add the ice water and minced garlic to the meat and fat mixture. Mix on the lowest setting of the stand mixer or by hand for 1 to 2 minutes until the mixture binds together. Place the meat in the fridge while you clean up.

4. Flush the sheep casings with warm water and set them aside.

5. Stuff the meat mixture into the sheep casings using a sausage stuffer, being careful not to overstuff them. Fill each casing with a link between 12 and 24 inches, leaving extra casing on both ends. Cut the casing and continue making links until all the meat is used.

6. Use a sterilized needle to pierce any air pockets in the casings. Gently squeeze the meat in the casings to tighten them. If any casings break, put the meat back into the stuffer and make another link. Once all the links are firm, tie the ends together with a double or triple knot and trim any excess casing.

7. Hang the links in a cool place for several hours to dry. If the temperature is 70°F (21°C) or above, hang them for only an hour.

8. Transfer the links to a smoker and smoke them until the interior reaches 150°F (66°C). Keep the smoker cool enough to achieve this in about 4 hours, allowing the links to absorb plenty of smoke.

9. Let the links cool, then find a cool, dark place with a temperature between 35°F (2°C) and 60°F (15°C) to hang them. Leave the links to dry for 3 to 5 days. They are now reasonably shelf-stable, but it's recommended to store them in the refrigerator. If you plan to keep them for longer than a month, wrap them tightly or vacuum seal and freeze.

DUTCH DROGE WORST

Ingredients:

- 9 kilograms of pork shoulder, 20% fat
- 1 kilogram of pork shoulder, 30% fat
- 10 grams of dry sausage seasoning mix per package
- Pork casings
- 25 grams of curing salt per kilogram

Instructions:

1. Soak the pork casings in plenty of cold water the day before and rinse them well before using.

2. Ensure that all the ingredients are cold, preferably close to frozen.

3. Grind the meat using the 5 mm plate.

4. Thoroughly mix the dry sausage seasoning mix and curing salt into the meat mixture.

5. Stuff the mixture into the pork casings, making sure to eliminate any air bubbles.

6. Hang the sausages in a dry place at around 20 degrees Celsius, preferably with some ventilation to allow any released moisture to escape.

7. Allow the sausages to dry for at least 2 weeks.

   Please note that curing and sausage-making can involve food safety risks, so it's essential to follow proper hygiene practices and consult reliable sources for detailed instructions.

MEXICAN CHORIZO SECO

Ingredients:

- 2 1/2 pounds (1.1 kg) pork venison, wild boar, bear, or other meat
- 10 ounces (280 g) pork fat
- 2 tablespoons plus 1 teaspoon (23 grams) kosher salt
- 1/4 teaspoon (3 grams) Instacure No. 1
- 1 heaping teaspoon (4 grams) sugar
- 2 teaspoons (4 grams) crushed black pepper
- 1 heaping teaspoon (2 grams) nutmeg
- 2 teaspoons (2 grams) caraway seed
- 1/4 teaspoon (1 gram) celery seed
- 4 cloves garlic, minced
- 1/3 cup (80 ml) ice water
- 20 feet sheep casings, soaked in tepid water

Instructions:

1. Soak the cleaned peppers (opened, without stems or seeds) in a bowl of hot water for about 30 minutes.

2. Grind the herbs and spices using a mortar and pestle or a small grinder, like a coffee grinder.

3. Blend the soaked peppers (without water), garlic cloves, and vinegar until you have a smooth purée. Set it aside.

4. Place the pork meat and fatback in a large bowl. Add the ground herbs and spices mixture and mix everything thoroughly. Then, add the purée and mix well to combine.

5. Note: At this point, you can make a small patty and fry it to taste and adjust the seasoning according to your preference.

6. Transfer the meat mixture to a container, preferably a glass one. Close the container tightly and let it cure in the refrigerator for one day. During this time, the flavors and aromas will blend and intensify.

7. After the curing time, remove the container from the refrigerator, give the mixture a little stir, and either divide it into small packages or stuff it into sausage casings. The chorizo can be frozen and stored for several months.

   HOW TO STUFF THE CHORIZO INTO CASINGS:

8. Soak the dried casings in warm water until they become soft and pliable (at least 1 hour).

9. Run warm water through the casings to remove any residual salt.

GREEK LOUKANIKO

Ingredients:

- 1 1/2 pounds lamb or venison trimmings
- 2 1/2 pounds pork or wild boar
- 1 pound pork fat
- 3 tablespoons kosher salt
- 1 teaspoon Instacure No. 1 (optional)
- 2 rounded tablespoons sugar
- 5 tablespoons minced fresh garlic
- 1 tablespoon ground coriander seed

- 1 tablespoon cracked black pepper
- 2 tablespoons fennel seeds
- 1 tablespoon crushed dried oregano
- 2 teaspoons dried thyme
- 3 tablespoons grated fresh orange zest
- 1/2 cup white or red wine
- Hog casings

Instructions:

1. Chop the pork and lamb into rough chunks. Mix in the salt, curing salt (if using), and sugar, then grind the mixture through a coarse grinder die. Place it in the fridge overnight if possible, or for at least an hour, to help the sausage bind.

2. Set aside half of the coriander, black pepper, and fennel seeds in a small bowl. Soak the hog casings in warm water and chill the wine in the fridge. Ensure all your grinding equipment is cold.

3. Mix the remaining spices with the meat and fat, then grind the mixture a second time into a bowl. You can choose to grind it coarse or fine, depending on your preference. If the room temperature is above 70.F, set the bowl of meat in another bowl filled with ice. Once ground, transfer the meat to the freezer and clean up.

4. Use a stand mixer with the heavy paddle attachment or mix the meat by hand in a large container. Add the orange zest, reserved spices, and wine to the meat mixture. Mix well for about 2 minutes until it forms a sticky and cohesive paste. If mixing by hand, make sure your hands are cold.

5. Take out the sausage stuffer, ensuring it has been chilled in the fridge or freezer for a few hours. Fit it with the appropriate tube and stuff the sausage mixture into the casings all at once, before twisting it into links.

6. To twist the links, start at one end and compress the meat into the casing, then tie off the casing. Measure out a good-sized link, pinch it with your fingers, and repeat for the next link down the coil. Twist several times to tighten each link well. Repeat this process for all the links, and tie off the final link after compressing it.

7. Prick any air pockets using a sterilized needle and gently compress the meat in the casings to fill the pockets. Be careful not to rupture the casing while doing this.

8.

9. Hang the sausages to dry for approximately 2 hours in a room with a normal temperature. If the room is warmer than 75F, hang them for only 1 hour. Ideally, hang the links overnight at around 40F.

ROMANIAN SIBIU SALAMI

Ingredients:

- 700 g lean pork (1.54 lb)
- 300 g back fat (0.66 lb)
- Ingredients per 1000 g (1 kg) of meat:
- 30 g salt (5 tsp)
- 5.0 g Cure #2 (1 tsp)
- 2.0 g Dextrose (1/2 tsp)
- 2.0 g Sugar (1/2 tsp)
- 4.0 g Pepper (2 tsp)
- 1.0 g Garlic powder (1/2 tsp)
- 15 ml Red wine (1 tbsp)
- 0.12 g T-SPX culture (use scale)
- Mold 600 (Penicillium nalgiovense)

Instructions:

1. Grind the lean meat using a 3-4 mm plate.

2. Cut the fat into 3-4 mm cubes.

3. 30 minutes before mixing, dissolve the starter culture in 15 ml of de-chlorinated water.

4. Mix the lean pork with salt and cure #2. Add the spices and culture. Mix well. Add the diced fat and mix everything together.

5. Stuff the mixture firmly into 60-90 mm horse or collagen casings, making 20-30 cm (8-12 inch) straight links. Clip or tie both ends.

6. Dry the sausages for 24 hours at 10-15°C (50-59°F) with moderate air circulation.

7. Apply cold smoke at 10-24°C (50-75°F) for 3 to a maximum of 10 days, with a relative humidity of 85 to 92%. Use oak, beech, or a mixture of both woods for smoking. The smoking does not have to be continuous, as long as the low temperature is maintained. Cold smoking is drying with smoke, and fermentation takes place during this step.

8. Once no more smoke is applied (smoke prevents the growth of mold), spray the sausages with Penicillium nalgiovense mold growing culture. Maintain the temperature at 10-24°C (50-75°F) and humidity at 85% for about 10-12 days.

9. When the sausages are completely covered with white, grey, or white-yellow mold, manually brush them to create a better look and facilitate drying. Then, let the sausages dry/mature at 10-15°C (50-59°F) for about 60 days. As the drying continues, lower the humidity.

10. Store the sausages at 10-12°C (50-55°F) with a humidity of 60-70%.

BELGIAN ARDENNES

Ingredients:

- 700 g pork shoulder
- 300 g back fat (pork belly)
- Ingredients per 1000 g (1 kg) of meat:
- 28 g salt (5 tsp)
- 2.5 g Cure #2 (1/2 tsp)
- 3.0 g Dextrose (1/2 tsp)
- 2.0 g Sugar (1/2 tsp)
- 1.0 g Cumin (1/2 tsp)
- 0.5 g Nutmeg (1/4 tsp)
- 3.5 g Garlic (1 clove)
- 1.0 g crushed Juniper berries (1 tsp)
- 0.12 g T-SPX culture (use scale)

Instructions:

1. Grind the pork shoulder using a 6 mm plate.

2. Grind the back fat (pork belly) using a 6 mm plate.

3. 30 minutes before mixing, dissolve the starter culture in 15 ml of de-chlorinated water.

4. Mix the pork shoulder with salt and cure #2. Add the spices and culture. Mix well. Add the ground fat and mix everything together.

5. Stuff the mixture firmly into 40 mm hog casings.

6. Ferment at 20°C (68°F) for 72 hours, with a humidity of 85-90%.

7. Apply a thin cold smoke at 18°C (64°F) for 2 days. The smoking does not have to be continuous as long as the temperature is maintained. Oakwood or beech wood can be used. Juniper berries (not wood or twigs) may be added to the fire as well.

8. Dry at 15°C to 12°C (59°F to 53°F), with a humidity of 65-75%, for 3 weeks, or until the sausage loses at least 20% of its original weight after stuffing.

9. Store the sausages at 10°C to 12°C (50°F to 55°F), with a humidity below 75%.

The raw material can consist of either pork or a combination of pork and beef. If using beef, it should not exceed 40% of the total wet weight of the raw material.
The sausage can come in three forms: long (30 and 90 mm diameter, maximum length of 60 cm), collar (ring) with a diameter of 20-40 mm, or short (30 mm diameter, 15 cm long).

DANISH RØD PØLSE

Ingredients:

350 g veal or beef
350 g pork
300 g pork back fat
Ingredients per 1000 g (1 kg) of meat:
18 g salt (3 tsp)
2.5 g Cure #1 (1/2 tsp)
2.0 g pepper (1 tsp)
1.0 g coriander (1/2 tsp)
0.5 g nutmeg (1/4 tsp)
0.5 g ginger (1/4 tsp)
60 ml water (2 fl oz)

Instructions:

Grind the pork through a 6 mm plate.

Grind the pork back fat through a 6 mm plate.

Grind the veal or beef through a 3 mm plate.

Using a food processor, emulsify the beef and pork with salt, cure #1, and water. Add the fat and spices, and emulsify everything together.

Stuff the mixture into 26 mm sheep casings, making 15 cm (6") links. Let them sit at room temperature for 1 hour.

Smoke the sausages at 60°C (140°F) for 1 hour.

Cook the sausages in water at 80°C (176°F) for 25 minutes.

Immerse the cooked sausages in cold water to which a food-approved red coloring has been added for 10 minutes.

Briefly dry the sausages and then refrigerate them.

For a stronger color, you can add a food-approved red coloring to the water while cooking the sausages.

SWEDISH SALSICCIA

Ingredients:

- 500 g pork shoulder
- 300 g pork back fat
- 20 g salt
- 5 g ground white pepper
- 5 g ground ginger
- 5 g ground nutmeg
- 2 g ground allspice
- 1 g ground cloves
- 100 ml ice-cold water
- Hog casings

Instructions:

1. Cut the pork shoulder and back fat into small pieces and place them in a bowl. Make sure the ingredients are very cold.

2. Grind the pork shoulder and back fat separately using a meat grinder fitted with a medium plate.

3. In a large mixing bowl, combine the ground pork shoulder, ground back fat, salt, white pepper, ginger, nutmeg, allspice, and cloves. Mix well until all the ingredients are evenly distributed.

4. Gradually add the ice-cold water to the mixture while continuously mixing. The water will help bind the ingredients together and keep the sausages moist.

5. Prepare the hog casings by rinsing them thoroughly and soaking them in water according to the package instructions.

6. Stuff the sausage mixture into the hog casings using a sausage stuffer or a sausage attachment for a meat grinder. Twist the sausages to form individual links, making sure they are tightly packed but not overstuffed.

7. Once all the sausages are stuffed and linked, refrigerate them for at least 1 hour to allow the flavors to develop and the sausages to firm up.

8. When ready to cook, you can either grill the sausages over medium heat or pan-fry them in a little oil until they are nicely browned and cooked through.

9. Serve the Swedish Salsiccia sausages hot with your choice of accompaniments, such as mashed potatoes, lingonberry sauce, and pickled cucumbers.

Russian Kielbasa

Ingredients:

- 700 g pork shoulder
- 300 g beef chuck
- 200 g pork back fat
- 20 g salt
- 5 g ground black pepper
- 5 g garlic powder
- 5 g mustard seeds
- 2 g ground coriander
- 1 g ground allspice
- 1 g ground nutmeg
- 100 ml ice-cold water
- Hog casings

Instructions:

1. Cut the pork shoulder, beef chuck, and pork back fat into small pieces and place them in a bowl. Ensure that the ingredients are well chilled.

2. Grind the pork shoulder, beef chuck, and pork back fat separately using a meat grinder fitted with a medium plate.

3. In a large mixing bowl, combine the ground pork shoulder, beef chuck, and pork back fat. Add the salt, black pepper, garlic powder, mustard seeds, coriander, allspice, and nutmeg. Mix well until all the ingredients are evenly distributed.

4. Gradually add the ice-cold water to the mixture while continuously mixing. The water helps bind the ingredients together and keeps the sausages moist.

5. Prepare the hog casings by rinsing them thoroughly and soaking them in water according to the package instructions.

6. Stuff the sausage mixture into the hog casings using a sausage stuffer or a sausage attachment for a meat grinder. Twist the sausages to form individual links, making sure they are tightly packed but not overstuffed.

7. Once all the sausages are stuffed and linked, refrigerate them for at least 1 hour to allow the flavors to develop and the sausages to firm up.

8. To cook the Russian Kielbasa sausages, you can either grill them over medium heat or pan-fry them in a little oil until they are nicely browned and cooked through.

9. Serve the Russian Kielbasa sausages hot with your choice of accompaniments, such as sauerkraut, mustard, and crusty bread.

Ukrainian Salo Sausage

Ingredients:

- 1 kg pork back fat (salo)
- 20 g salt
- 5 g ground black pepper
- 5 g crushed garlic
- 2 g paprika (optional)
- 1 g dried thyme (optional)
- Hog casings

Instructions:

1. Cut the pork back fat into small cubes or strips, ensuring that it is well chilled.

2. In a large mixing bowl, combine the pork back fat with salt, black pepper, crushed garlic, paprika (if using), and dried thyme (if using). Mix well until all the ingredients are evenly distributed.

3. Allow the mixture to marinate in the refrigerator for about 1 hour to let the flavors meld together.

4. Meanwhile, prepare the hog casings by rinsing them thoroughly and soaking them in water according to the package instructions.

5. After marinating, start stuffing the sausage mixture into the hog casings using a sausage stuffer or a sausage attachment for a meat grinder. Make sure to fill the casings evenly and avoid overstuffing.

6. Once all the sausages are stuffed, twist or tie them at regular intervals to create individual links. Ensure that the links are secure but not too tight.

7. Hang the sausages in a cool and well-ventilated area for about 12-24 hours to allow them to dry and develop their flavor. You can use a sausage drying rack or a clean, dry area with good air circulation.

8. After drying, the Ukrainian Salo sausages are ready to be enjoyed. They can be eaten as they are, thinly sliced and served as a snack or appetizer.

9. Store any remaining sausages in the refrigerator in a sealed container or wrapped in wax paper.

   Note: Traditional Ukrainian Salo sausages are typically consumed without cooking, as they are cured and air-dried. However, if desired, you can lightly pan-fry or grill the sausages until they are crispy on the outside and heated through.

SWISS CERVELAT

Ingredients:

700 g pork trimmings
200 g lean beef
100 g pork back fat
Ingredients per 1000g (1 kg) of meat:
28 g salt
5.0 g cure #2
5.0 g sugar
2.0 g black pepper
2.0 g sweet paprika
1.0 g ground coriander

Instructions:

- Take a piece of skinless back fat and evenly rub it with 5% salt (50 g salt per 1 kg of back fat) on all sides. Place it in the refrigerator at 4 C (40 F) for 2 weeks. Rinse the fat with cold water to remove any crystallized salt. Cut it into 1/2" (12 mm) cubes.

- Grind the pork using a 3/8" (10 mm) plate.

- Grind the beef using a 1/8" (3 mm) plate.

- In a large mixing bowl, combine the ground pork, ground beef, back fat cubes, salt, cure #2, sugar, black pepper, sweet paprika, and ground coriander. Mix well until all the ingredients are evenly distributed.

- Pack the mixture tightly into a container that is approximately 6" (15 cm) deep. Place it in the refrigerator and let it sit for 4 days.

- Stuff the sausage mixture firmly into hog bungs, beef middles, or large diameter synthetic protein-lined fibrous casings, according to your preference.

- Hang the sausages in a cool and well-ventilated area for 3 weeks at 10 C (50 F) to allow them to dry.

- After the drying period, apply cold smoke at 18 C (68F) for 2 days.

- Store the sausages at 10-12 C (50-53 F) until they are ready to be enjoyed.

Austrian Landjäger

Ingredients:

- 700 g pork
- 300 g lean beef
- Ingredients per 1000g (1 kg) of meat:
- 28 g salt
- 2.5 g cure #2
- 3.0 g dextrose
- 3.0 g pepper
- 2.0 g cumin
- 1.0 g nutmeg
- 0.12 g T-SPX culture (use scale)

Instructions:

1. Grind the pork using a 5 mm (1/4") plate. Grind the beef using a 3 mm (1/8") plate.

2. In a large mixing bowl, combine the ground pork, ground beef, salt, cure #2, dextrose, pepper, cumin, nutmeg, and T-SPX culture. Mix well to evenly distribute the ingredients.

3. Stuff the mixture loosely into 32-36 mm hog casings, filling them to about 80% capacity. Make individual links that are approximately 8" (20 cm) long. Place the stuffed sausages between two boards with some weight on top to flatten them slightly. Then transfer them to a fermentation room.

4. Ferment the sausages at 20o C (68° F) for 72 hours, maintaining a humidity level of 95-90%.

5. Remove the boards and wipe off any slime that may have accumulated underneath.

6. Allow the sausages to dry at room temperature until the casings are dry to the touch. Hang the square-shaped sausages on smoke sticks.

7. Apply cold smoke at a temperature below 20o C (68o F) for a few hours to prevent the growth of mold.

8. Continue drying the sausages at 14-12° C (58-54° F) with a humidity level of 85-80% for approximately 3 weeks, or until the sausages have lost around 30% of their original weight.

9. Store the sausages at 10-12° C (50-53° F) with a humidity level below 75%.

IRISH BLACK PUDDING

Ingredients:

- 2 liters Pigs Blood (8 1/2 cups)
- 500 g Diced Pig Fat (or suet) (18 oz)
- 250 g Sliced Onions (finely diced) (9 oz)
- 2 tbsp Oatmeal (soaked overnight)
- 1 tsp White Pepper
- 1 tsp Instacure No. 1
- 1/2 tsp Coriander
- 1/4 tsp Cumin
- 1/4 tsp Ground Cloves
- 500 ml Milk or Heavy Cream (2 cups)
- Natural Hog Casings

Instructions:

1. Fry onion in a skillet with a touch of lard over low-medium heat until carmelized. Remove and cool, you can do this a day in advance if you want.

2. In a small bowl combine oatmeal, salt, pepper, coriander, cumin, cloves. Set aside.

3. Start with frozen, or partially frozen fat to make life easier and dice it up. Coat the pork with the seasoning mixture.

4. Place the blood and coated pork fat into the freezer and allow it to get nice and cold while you soak your hog casings.

5. Once everything has soaked and got nice and cold (you'll want it roughly 35F), you'll want to start mixing everything together. Using the paddle attachment on your stand mixer, or a nice, big spoon if you don't have one, combine the fat, oats, milk, and blood by adding the blood in just a bit at a time (a cup or so). Continue mixing on low until everything is well combined. It will likely appear there has been a massacre.

6. Prepare a large pot of boiling water and get it boiling on the stove while everything is mixing up.

7. Thread the sausage stuffer with your hog casing and begin pouring the mixture into your stuffer. You will want to make an entire coil before you tie into links, and you do need to tie the ends off with butcher's twine.

8. Gently lower the sausages into the pot of boiling water one at a time. Poach for 15-20 minutes. You can check to see if it is done by pricking it with a needle, if the liquid that escapes is brown, it is finished.

9. While poaching, prepare a bowl of ice water to blanch them in. Once they have finished, immediately plunge them into the ice water. Once cool, remove and allow them to dry out for about an hour.

10. They can be served cold or fried.

AMERICAN PEPPERONI

Ingredients:

- 2 kg ground pork
- 900 g ground beef
- 115 g Pepperoni Seasoning*
- 7 g cure (comes with the seasoning)*
- 180 ml water, plus more as needed
- 1–3 drops liquid smoke (optional)
- 2–3 tsp. crushed red pepper flakes (optional)

Instructions:

1. In a mixing bowl, combine the ground pork and ground beef.

2. Add the Pepperoni Seasoning to the meat mixture and mix well.

3. Dissolve the cure in 180 ml of water. If desired, add liquid smoke and crushed red pepper flakes to the water.

4. Pour the cure mixture into the meat mixture and mix thoroughly by hand. Add more water, 1 teaspoon at a time, until the mixture becomes sticky enough to stick to an inverted hand.

5. Stuff the meat mixture into casings using a sausage stuffer according to the manufacturer's instructions. Alternatively, follow alternative methods for making sausage without special equipment.

6. Refrigerate the sausages, whether in casings or wrapped in plastic wrap and foil, in a single layer for 24 hours to allow the cure to penetrate and for the shape of the sausages to set.

7. Preheat the oven to 165°C.

8. If using plastic wrap and foil, carefully remove them from the sausages. Place the sausages, or the casings stuffed with meat, on an oven-safe rack placed over a baking sheet.

9. Bake in the preheated oven for 45-60 minutes, or until the internal temperature of the meat reaches 71°C when measured with an instant-read thermometer.

10. Remove from the oven and let the sausages cool.

11. Slice and enjoy.

We kindly invite you to share your thoughts and feedback about the book by leaving a review on Amazon. Your opinion matters to us, and it helps other readers discover and appreciate the book as well. We value your feedback and appreciate your time in writing a review. Thank you for being a part of our reading community and for supporting authors like us. Happy reading

Made in the USA
Coppell, TX
29 November 2023

24950094R00070